Poems From My Heart

Myles W. Wallace

Order this book online at www.trafford.com
or email orders@trafford.com

Most Trafford titles are also available at major online book retailers.

Printed in the United States of America.

ISBN: 978-1-4907-2976-3 (sc)
ISBN: 978-1-4907-2977-0 (e)

Trafford rev. 03/04/2014

Trafford PUBLISHING® www.trafford.com
North America & international
toll-free: 1 888 232 4444 (USA & Canada)
fax: 812 355 4082

In God We Trust

This book is dedicated with Love to my wife Sybil
and our daughter Mya

Contents

10-4

I had an argument with my baby, last night
It seems lately
All we do, is fuss and fight

I asked her, what's the problem?
She said; it's me
I thought it was her
Together we are incomplete

I left the house, thinking when life was roses
When I returned, she was standing in the door
Expecting to greet with a kisses and hugs
As we had done before
Instead, with pouted lips
She said; 10-4
Baby, I don't want you no more

I was stunned, can we work it out
I pleaded
My lady wouldn't hear it
Oh No!
Shook her head vigorously
10-4
Sir, you've got to go!

She loudly repeated
10-4
Shut the door
Man, you've got to go

I left—immediately
Tears swelled eyes
It was too hard to believe
After many happy years
My love she denied

When I call
The phone she refuses to answer
Letters return unopened
I felt our love would always be everlasting

Friends tell her
How much she means to me
Words that fall on deaf ears
My love she just won't see

If we don't get back together
I just want you to know
Darling, your love will always be in my heart
You're the only star in my show

I miss you honey
That's a sweet 10-4

24-7

24-7, I want to make our love better
24-7, I want to make our love better

I want to make our love better
12 months in the year
52 weeks per annual
365 days a year
Leap year makes it better

In short I am saying
24-7, I want to make our love better
I will keep you happy 24-7
I want to make our love better

I will love you
8760 hours in the year
525,600 minutes per annual
31,536,000 seconds a year
With one extra day for 4 calendars

I will make our love hot and caring
24-7, I want to make our love better
Just you and me sharing
24-7, I will make our love better

26 Love

It's 26 Love
Becoming a woman from a girl
26 Love
The way of her world

He is forty-something
She 26
He falls in love
It's not her mix

Experience brings patience
He keeps trying
She avoids him
Persistence he is plying

It's 26 Love
Her way of maturation
26 Love
For him more than infatuation

He won't give up
It is not his nature
She keeps resisting
Gives him more flavor

A man chases a woman
Till she catches him
This race he wishes
She definitely wins

28 You're Great!

At 25 you were more than qualified
For 26 your talents inflated
Then 27 you became even better
Now—28 you're great!

Darling, there is no limit
For goals you want to accomplish
May these words serve as
Words of encouragement

From college you will graduate
After obtaining your PHD
For that ceremony you will be chauffeured in
Your brand-new red convertible jeep cherokee!

Whatever you set your mind for
It always comes true
There is never turning back
For the quests you want to do

Honey, keep on keeping on
I admire your determination, your heart
You never give up
You dismiss the word hard

Congratulations, sweetheart
For any target achieved
I will be your unwavering supporter
With any idea you conceive

I toast your performance
Success knows your place
For the best in life
Darling, at 28 you're great!

50-100 = 50

So you will live to be one-hundred
50 of those are gone
You chase young girls
While you leave your wife at home

Mother Nature has got you
Father Time soon will
There is nowhere to go
Except downhill

50-100 = 50
Check your math
50-100 = 50
Better do it fast

The previous three decades
You thought you were king
Then you were rudely awakened
With one last fling

You destroyed another life
Leaving behind a baby
Now that you are finished
It is home to the old lady

50-100 = 50
Your life is about over
50-100 = 50
See the bells tolling

A Man Can't Do Nothing For Me

I was born in Chicago
A city founded by a black man
My ancestors emigrated from Africa
The Motherland

A black man fathered me
A black midwife delivered me
A black woman raised me
I was the first son born
Twelve midnight, at home

I began work at the age of five
Planting black eye peas
And blackberries
In my daddy's black yard

When I started school
My kindergarten teacher was black
So was my opponent
In my first grade fight

A man can't do nothing for me
Except pay me on time
No man can do nothing for me
While I taste my sweet black wine

My wife is black
Obviously the children
The dog is black
Uh, he's a french poodle

My home is painted black
So is the furniture
My car is black
Like the road down under

I like to dine on black bread with black beans
Followed by chocolate milk and blackberry pie
At my black table
Using my black fork and black knife

Once a week I read Jet
I subscribe to the Defender
I really dig Players
Ebony is my favorite

Walter Payton was my favorite football player
Michael Jordan was my favorite basketball player
Willie Mays was my favorite baseball player
Eddie Robinson belongs with the pros

Now, I am my own boss
Where I gig
So are my black security men
Who guard my black machines

A man can't do nothing for me
Except mind his own business
No man can do nothing for me
There are no exceptions

A Spark Of Your Love

A spark of your love
Is like thunder from above
A spark of your love
Puts lightning in my heart
One flick of your bic
Like pow!—It does the trick

You turn me on and
I can't turn me off
Like a doorknob
I feel boss

A spark of your love
Is a dose from above
Lightning, thunder, fire
All in one

You are lightning without pain
Thunder without rain and
Fire without smoke

A spark of your love
Inspired me to write this song

Myles W. Wallace

A Winter Night On A Summer Day

Though the sun shined brightly above
A cold wind blew, I lost my love
The heat was hot in the air
My heart didn't seem to care

It was a winter night on a summer day
Yes, it was a winter night on a summer day

As the birds sang in the breeze
A dark cloud hovered—believe
The trees lulled tawny and tight
While the light of day turned into night

It was a winter night on a summer day
Yes, it was a winter night on a summer day

As the bees buzzed back and forth
A cold chill rushed through my throat
The smell of sweet honey went round and round
All I could do was frown

It was a winter night on a summer day
It was a winter night on a summer day

The ocean swept in and in
All I could manage was a tear
As the moon crept through the clouds
My feeling for you could not be bound

It was a winter night on a summer day
Oh, it was a winter night on a summer day

Accept My Love

Accept my love
Don't grade it
Try to shade it
If you want
You can praise

Accept my love
Don't deny it
Say goodbye to it
If you can
Try to rely on it

Accept my love
Don't toy with it
Destroy it
If you wish
You can buoy from it

Accept my love
Don't judge it
Fudge it
Live with it
You can not budge it

Accept my love
Don't dodge it
Play hodgepodge with it
You can have it
Any time you want it

Accept my love
Don't play with it
Escape from it
If you can
Try to stay with it

Accept my love
Enjoy it
Have fun with it
It is for a life time
Take care of it

Accept my love
Keep it
Don't peep it
If you must
Release it

Accept my love
Don't boss it
Toss it
If you are aware
There is no cost for it

Accept my love
Don't cuss it
Don't fuss with it
Are you willing
To surrender to it

Accept my love
Don't fight it
Don't bite it
If you want
Invite it

Accept my love
Don't lose it
Use it
When you can
Groove to it

Accept my love
Don't force it
Distant it
Be resistant to it
Put a voice with it

Accept my love
Don't break it
Shake it
Have faith in it
Together we can make it

"Ace"

He is my good ole buddy, my homie
I call him Bo
He is my partner
With favors to go

When I'm down
He won't let me go out
He is always near
To lift me up

"Ace"
My friend
"Ace"
My main man

When we're out on the town
He watches my back
He won't let anyone
Disturb the night

If I need money
I can depend on him
He always has
A helping hand

"Ace"
On time
"Ace"
The bottom line

Airhead

You say one thing
Then do another
You don't know if you are
Talking to a sister or a brother

You put money in the bank
Then forget you deposited it
You don't understand
Your clothes belong in the closet

You call a neighbor
Then hang up in mid-sentence
Was it a cat or a dog
You don't know the difference

You're an airhead
Just flowing through life
Say airhead
Don't take flight

You have conversations
And forget what you said
Most of the time
You're on the wrong side of the bed

You dream about the lotto
Then think that you have won
You realize you forgot to play
Because you had no funds

You try to make life
A startling revelation
Then you find out
You are in a messed up situation

Airhead, you're going out the world
Backwards, as it has been said before
You're always on the wrong side
Of a vaulted door

Airhead,
One day at a time
Ok, airhead
Now, hold the line

Anger

Anger spreads through your body
It touches every nerve
It reveals in your face
Like land in a flood

Anger like in danger
Takes you out of control
It stops you from thinking
A downhill roll

Anger is madness
Anger is fury, indignation, ire
Anger is wrath and rage
Anger is playing with fire

Anger is selfish, stupid and dull
Anger is foolish, silly, absurd
Anger gets you nowhere
To get angry is just plain dumb

Try love as an alternative
Love yourself
Love your neighbor
Love the universe
Put anger to rest

Attraction

It's true, I want more
Than to be a friend
When we met, my love began

A relationship should grow
With kisses and hugs
For you sweetheart
I want the stars above

Darling, I'm attracted to you
Like poles on a magnet
For you, I have a strong reaction

Sugar, I'm attracted to you
Like coffee and cream
Together we could blend

Your personality drew me hear
Your warmth keeps me near

Sweetheart I'm attracted to you
Like lightning to a rod
Lady, you struck my heart

Honey, I'm attracted to you
Like a bee to a flower
Your love is sweet power

B. S. (Bad Sister)

I scoped her from my window
As she was strutting her stuff
The fellows on the corner
Could not get enough

I ran down the stairs
To take a closer look
When I got there
My heart went, up my throat

The lady walked like a goddess
She flowed as if she were a queen
My eyes were transfixed
This woman was keen

I said to myself
Oh B.S. This is a bad sister
Then I hollered out
"B.S. This is one bad sister"

I knew I was not going to
Let her get away
After all, this fine lady
Just made my day

I caught up with her
I began to chat
I asked her name
She was indecisive
Kind of matter-of-fact

After a minute or two
The word rolled off her lips
Like sweetened honey
I felt as if
I was having a second coming

I stood back and gasped
"B.S. You are a bad sister"
I could only stand fast and say
"B.S. I mean you are a bad sister"

She told me
She was on her way to the store
And If it wasn't an inconvenience
Did I care to go

I didn't want this opportunity
To pass me by
It would be like getting hit in the face
With a whipped cream pie

As we walked,
I asked her
Could I hold her hand
When she obliged
I thought I was in never, never, land

I yelled out
"Oh B.S. You are a bad sister"
Then I shouted
"On man! B.S. You are a real bad sister"

After we made the run
The only one for that day
I looked at her
I started saying

"You know doll,"
"I have waited my life for you"
"I cannot let you get away"
"You are my dream come true"
"We compliment each other"
"In so many ways"

She laid her head on my shoulder
As she was softly saying
"I am not going anywhere"
"Here I am and here I'll stay"

I said: "Oh! B.S. You know you are bad sister"
That is why I serenade
She said: "Oh B.S. I know I am a bad sister"
"I am the only star in your parade"

B.Y.O.B. Bring Your Own Baby

We go to a party
And before I can sit down
My lady is up
Dancing with a dude
Who thinks he knows the town

They dance fast
Then the music slows
In my presence
Romeo doesn't want to let go

My lady doesn't want to be rude
Just trying to have fun
It becomes quite difficult
To ignore a persistent Don Juan

Whatever she requests
He's johnny-on-the-spot
He is her gopher
Non-stop

This is what I say
While I regain control
The lady is with me
Man, stop being so bold

B.Y.O.B.—Bring your own baby
Leave mine for me
B.Y.O.B.—Bring your own baby
At the count of three

There are plenty of women, here
Let mine be
If you don't
Daylight you won't see

I know my lady looks good
That's one reason I brought her here
Now, turn her loose
Let her swing

Don't get me wrong
I'm not here to start trouble
But, if you don't stop
You'll have a busted bubble

B.Y.O.B.—Bring your own baby
Plenty are free
B.Y.O.B.—Get your own lady
Just try, you'll see

Bad Head

The liqueur was gushing
It was one continuous flow
Its final destination was
Right beneath my nose

The bartender shouted
"I'm ready to close!"
I said: "What the heck
Give me one for the road!"

I escaped to my car
Somehow I made it home
I don't remember how I got there
Or who opened the door

I woke up the next morning
With a throbbing in my brain
I started arguing with myself
I don't think I was sane

Right then and there
I gave up the grog
Two days later
My mind was still a fog

Bad head
Once was enough for me
A bad head is
Totally incapacitating

Bailout

When a situation
Takes you near the brink
When you don't take time to
Stop and think
-Bailout

When the going gets tough
And you're not tough enough
To keep going-
When you're going down fast
Because you don't feel like growing
-Bailout

Is it worth all
The pain and trouble
When the only thing to gain
Is abundant courage?
-Bailout

Everyday can be a challenge
When times get hard
If you don't have patience
-Bailout and run

If you can't take it anymore
The pressure seems too great
Follow your prepared plan
For your great escape
-Bailout

Bankshot (Pool Shark)

He shot the ball
It was not a game of bumper
The eight ball
Ricocheted off a cushion
A real hard thumper

The blackball weaved
Through a forest maze
The destination entrance
Passed along the way

The inky ball circled the table
In little dippy dos
It bounded back and forth and
Made a couple of loops

His bankshot was ball control
The bankshot was total resolve

With a choice of six holes
The ball had eyes
For the corner slot
To win the game
Down the dark ball plopped

Bankshot was king clout
Bankshot won the master bout

Battlefield Promotion

Woman you have stood by me
Through thick and thin
You have fought with me
When I thought I could never win

From everyday confrontations
To all out warfare
I could depend on you
To always be there

I am going to give you
A battlefield promotion
General of the family
You are a five star wonder
For life that you handle

You do not use weapons
Just your clever charm
Any volatile situation
You can disarm

You never use threats
Or deceptive tactics
Your philosophy is to act
Not to start attacking

You will not use propaganda
You just say what you feel and
No matter how explosive the setting
You can always strike a deal

You deserve a battlefield promotion
A Medal of Honor
That is only the beginning
For your love, dedication, devotion

Beauty And The Beast

She wears long flowing gowns
Hair sprinkled queen
Her wrists are wrapped with gold
Fingers covered in rings

Roll out the red carpet
Sound the trumpet-horns
Her feet never touch the ground
A genuine celebrity star

Beauty and the beast
The perfect lady—huh?
She's beauty and the beast
I'll tell you why

She'll chew me out
At the drop of a hat
Talk about me
My dog and cat

She will not do anything
I ask her to do
If I ask her why
She will cut me loose

Beauty and the beast
Dr. Jekyll and Mrs. Hyde
Beauty and the beast
From me she cannot hide

Better Safe, Than Sorry

See the hitchhiker
Thumbing a ride
Press the gas
Pass him by

Look at the people
Peddling wares
Keep your money
Don't take a chance

Better safe, than sorry
It's better to say
There he goes, instead of
There he lays

If you see a person
Blocking your path
Stop and look
For another path

If you want to party
At some far out place
Take a rain check
To save face

Better safe, than sorry
Is the only way
Better safe, than sorry
Is the best fate

Black Knight

He races through coal mines
Like black silk
He makes dark powder
Out of chocolate milk

Like the Ace-of-Spades
He is the head
Shadows of darkness
Cloak his bed

The Black Knight-
Ebony man
Black Knight
Has secret plans

He rides a sable stallion
Only at dusk
He wears charcoal garb
Pitched jack boots
With jet-leather gloves

Like that old magic
His program is ink
He is stormy weather
No time to blink

Black Knight-
Cimmerian man
The Black Knight has
Swarthy plans

Boot Knocker

He travels the world
He's no Bee Bopper
Just a man full of love
His name: Boot Knocker

He knocks boots in the East
He knocks boots in the West
He knocks boots both day and night
Boot Knocker does his best

Ladies idolize him
Men admire him too
Boot Knocker has a lot of charm
He'll even knock it with two

The Boot Knocker—Knocks
The Boot Knocker—Socks
The Boot Knocker—Rocks
Boot Knocker—Don't stop

Ladies, Boot Knocker is coming soon
To your part of town
Show him a pretty smile
If you want Knocker to get down
Make him feel good
He might stay around

The Boot Knocker—Rocks
The Boot Knocker—Socks
Boot Knocker—Don't stop
Boot Knocker—Rock

The Boot Knocker has fun
While he pleases the ladies
When he visits you
Join him; The man is fascinating

Boot Knocker—Don't stop
The Boot Knocker—Rocks
The Boot Knocker—Knocks
Knocker—Really knows how to pop

Can I Be Sure

Can I be sure
That our love is true

Can I be sure
It's not all me and part of you

I must be sure
That our love is strong
A yearning my heart has longed

We must be positive
For our love to survive
This is truth and cannot be revised

Will this dilemma possess
The greatest love anyone knows yet

When we emerge with success
We will be sure
Our love was always best

Chaos

The way you answer the phone
Something is amiss
Your voice is erratic
Turmoil persists

I hear loud yelling
Tell me it's my imagination
Clamoring in the background
You say it's the television

It's chaos,
Your life it has surrounded
Chaos,
With drenching power

When the door bell rings
People begin to scramble
They figure it's the law
Coming in to gather

You can't maintain friends
With your troubled schemes
You insist you're getting over
Pinch yourself, you're dreaming

Chaos,
A no plot soap opera
Chaos,
Makes you inoperable

Cinderella-Baby

When they brought her in the room
The beacon was burning bright
It was the same light that guided
Mother-Melissa through the night

This little bundle of joy
Moments ago, the doctors delivered
Six pounds of charm
To God's fertile earth
A brand new addition

Baby's shiny eyes
Reveal a labor of love
Her delicate smile
Proof—there's God high above

Tiny hands
Reach out for the first taste of life
Unbound little feet
Prepare to take none tethered flight

She is a Cinderella—baby
Not because she was born
Past 12:00 in the night
She's a Cinderella child
Because she is a mother's dream
Cuddly, sweet, pure delight

Lauretta Jasmine Shenault
Was born to Melissa Shenault
In 1984, April 8

Procreated from her only child
She is Connie Duncan's first grandbaby

Sister Lauretta Pitts' second grandniece
After whom she was named

She is Mrs. Vivian Pitts' third greatgrandbaby
Without her none could claim

Most of all
Baby is a pretty little lady
A living doll
She is a Cinderella-baby

Before this beautiful baby was born
Melissa moved out of Mom's house
Mother and daughter were not on good terms
This wonderful child—convinced them
From each other, they could learn

They are very close now
Mother and daughter—an inseparable pair
Connie likes being baby's sitter
Watching preadolescence
Whose cute little dimples glow
Everytime she giggles

Into a strong woman
Baby Ja Ja will soon grow
The fourth generation of ladies
All in the know

The world will be her's
To reap from roots of knowledge
With her family beside
Academics she will brilliantly follow

In two decades
Perhaps slightly more
Baby Ja will establish precedence
She will excel
The fifth generation forth

Lauretta Jasmine Shenault
Some call her little Lo
Was born to Melissa Shenault
At St. Joseph's hospital
April 8, in the year 1984

She is Connie's first grandbabe
The sister of big Lo

She is Lauretta's greatniece
Who cherishes her more

She is Mrs. Vivian Pitts' greatgrandbaby
The number one star of the show

Most of all
She is happy and contented
A friendly, playful baby
A princess of a lady
Yes, she's God's special little lady
A Cinderella Baby

Class

It is not way you talk
But how you move your lips
It is not the way you walk
But how you sway your hips

It is the pleasing smile you have
That makes me do flips
It is how your eyes sparkle
That makes you so hep

Baby, you have class
You belong at the front of the line
Baby, you have class
Take your own sweet time

When we go out
You know exactly what to do
I don't have to say anything
You stay in the groove

Your position in life
Will always be the top
In my heart
You occupy the number one slot

Darling, you have class
In all ways you are right
Sweetheart, you have class
Your love is out-of-sight

Myles W. Wallace

Clever

He is a real hep dude
Who has been around
No one knows
This man about town

He is deceptively shy
Never has much to say
When the ladies talk
He looks the other way

Clever misses a wink
Clever catches with a blink

He dresses in
The 1990's style
His feet stand
On solid ground

His automobile is
The classy kind
His condominium
Just off lake shore drive

Clever is top of the line
Clever is right on time

Come

Hey baby, come with me
Let's have some fun
I don't want a crowd
Just you and me
One on one

Come with me in the morning
Come with me at night
Come with me easy
Don't be so tight

Come with me on the floor
Come with me against the wall
Come with me in the car
Come with me and have a ball

Come with me honey
I want you to scream
Come with me baby
In your tight blue jeans

Come with me on the table
Come with me in the chair
Come with me standing up
I am your teddy bear

Come with me on the stereo
Come with me on the speaker
Come with me to disco lights
Let's do it on the ceiling

Come with me on in the elevator
Come with me in Sears Tower
Come with me underground
Come hard with power

Come with me at the Court Supreme
Come with me in the space shuttle
Come with me on the Pacific Ocean
I'll heat you up, like a tea kettle

Come with me when the clock alarms
Come with me at midnight
Come with me in shadows
Stroke me in broad daylight

Come with me till there is no time
Come with me, sip some wine
Come with me, don't stop
Come with me, while I'm on top

Come with me sweetly, darling
Keep coming, love is running

Committed

I will stay by your side
Through thick and thin
I will be with you
From beginning to end

I will remain with you
When you rise to the top
I will not go anywhere
If the bottom drops out

Baby, I committed to you
Like oxygen to water
I am committed
As the earth is to orbit

If situations go wrong
I will make them right
At the end of the tunnel
Stands our guiding light

When all seems lost
I will help you recover
I will hold solid
When there is no other

Honey I am committed
To there is no time
Between you and me
There is no bottom line

Confessions

On the sofa we sit
My girl and me
I pull her close
To say something sweet

I tell her
Baby you are special to me
I love you sure

I observed you grow
From girl to woman
I view you mature

Confessions are special thoughts
Confessions are admired results

I always want to kiss you
You I love to caress
My joy was true in the past

As it is now
I am elated that
We are passionately involved

Confessions are secret feelings
Confessions are a heart revealing

Cowboy Love

I want to lasso you
Like Lash Larou
I want to corral your love
Like Wyatt Earp
And hold you too

I want you to be
My Annie Oakley
Fast on the love trigger
My probe of truth will
Enter you directly—evenly

I don't have to be the Lone Ranger
To scout your heart
I know you are beautiful
Like a sunset of roses
Better than Pocohantis

I want to be with you
Because, passion between us
Will be a lifetime of silver
I will be your Range Rider
Love we will keep on building

Darlin' Eyes

People say you have such a cute smile
They really dig the way you walk
They whisper about your unique style
And admire the way you talk

They rave, you're elegant—fashionable
High above the best
They continuously compliment you
About being prettier than the rest

Now, I'm in agreement
With all the things they say
But, what I like about you most
Accentuates your lovely face

It's those darlin' eyes
Sweet and divine
Baby, those darlin' eyes
Make you so delectably fine

You're a proud, independent woman
Intelligent, most self-assured
Quality is your motto
But, you are just as down-to-earth
To knock on wood

Your friends like where you're coming from
Inside your mind, they want to see
But, when they look into those gorgeous eyes
They know you're choice as love can be

Those dazzlin' darlin' eyes
They have such beautiful appeal
Because on your heart they rely
That's what makes you so for real

Darlin' eyes, I'm so proud
I want the whole world to see
This is just my way of saying
You are my living dream

Darling, You Will Always Be My Baby

As the sun rises
For earth's show
The moon shines
With rivers flow

Flowers bloom
From nectar bees
Woodwind compositions
By birds, in harmony

Darling, you will always be my baby
Joy you bring
Darling, you will always be my baby
Nature's Queen

Stars sparkle
In twinkled light
Meteors enhance
Lifes' delight

Night chimes
From melodic reeds
Futuristic scores
By rhythmic seeds

Darling, you will always be my baby
Sweetness you mean
Darling you will always be my baby
Top of cream

Date

We met at your place of work
Time set me in the right place
You captivated me with conversation
Which led to
Me asking you for a date

I planned the evening
Two weeks ahead
Baby, for you, fine lady
I wanted the best
Your beauty stayed in my head

I wished the date were today
I couldn't keep you off my mind
I counted every second
My heart beat time
Till we wined and dined

The day finally arrived
For the magnificent occasion
I was at your apartment
Promptly at nine o'clock
I greeted you with roses, trinkets and a teddy
You stood there blushing
I was more than ready

Darling, to put it bluntly
I was overpowered with your charm
Overwhelmed by your beauty
Right there, at that moment, in an instant
I knew I was in love

We proceeded to dinner
My head was in a cloud
I felt so good
You looked so pretty
I wanted shout out loud

When dinner was finished
We traveled to a live-band club
I asked you to dance
I wanted to hold you for life
I was even more in love

Nights always end
This one I never wanted to
The lights warmed up
We danced to the last song
I dedicated it to us
You were my dream come true

It was not over yet
I had to escort you home
That night, I savored every second
With one arm on the steering wheel
The other wrapped around you
I go the way-long

At your apartment door
We held each other tight
I didn't want to see you go
I asked for one more kiss
I loved your tenderness
Your affection I will miss

Darling, our date was more than a date
It was the beginning of a beautiful romance
I have cherished each moment we were together
Every touch, call, kiss takes me higher
A lifetime our date will last

Did You Ever Love Me

Did you ever love me
Did you even care
I can't believe
All in love is fair

Didn't you love me just a little
We were together one year
I know you liked me
You said have no fear

Did you ever love me
Just for one second
Can you ever love me
To breakup never

Please give me an answer
Your emotions I never questioned
I want to touch your tenderness
For your sweetness I am thirsty

My thoughts of you are constant
You are my heart
Of my life
You have become a part

Will you ever love me
As earth beats time
Would you ever love me
To share our minds

Don't Deny Me Your Love

Once we were tight
For reasons unknown, you changed
The love we had
Hardly knows my name

We met at a party
Had a good time
Then I walked you to the door
That's where you drew the line

When I call
First, you talk real nice
Then you hangup the phone
Before saying goodnight

Darling, don't deny me your love
You, I truly need
Don't deny me your love
You are my heartbeat

By coincidence
Our paths my cross
You slowdown to smile
But you refuse to talk

I send you letters
Never receive a reply
You tell my friends
I'm not your type

Don't deny me your love
With you, I am a winner
Don't deny me your love
Let's give love a new beginning

Don't Let Our Love End This Way

We shared many happy times together
Now you are gone
Memories of those sweet moments
Still linger on

He asked you to marry him
Before I ever had a chance
You took him up on his offer
Which ended our romance

Don't let our love end this way
You are constantly on my mind
Don't let our love end this way
Please don't let this be
The end of the line

I hope that you are satisfied
Now that you have made your choice
But I can't hold back the tears
There's an emptiness in my voice

I still see the diamond ring he gave you
Once the sparkle in my eyes
You even had his baby
My heart is empty as the darken sky

Don't let our love end this way
My body aches for your return
Don't let our love end this way
To you darling, my love belongs

Don't Send A Girl To Do A Woman's Job

Here is a man
With a job, house, car
Basic material possessions
He also has savings and checking accounts
He is single and he doesn't chase women

He wants to settle down
He meets a nice woman
His life use to be cozy
Since he met her
He doesn't know if he is
Coming or going

They plan dates well in advance
She stands him up
He is a forgiving person
So he calls her to see what happened
The phone she hangs up

She is younger than he
Hardly an excuse
They're both over eighteen
Adults the law says
She uses age as ruse

Don't send a girl to do a woman's job
It's best for her to stay home
Never send a girl to do woman's job
She should leave the situation alone

He attempts to talk with her
To see what's on her mind
There are times he throws up both hands
Walks and talks to himself
Hope he isn't wasting his time

She's a pretty lady
He hopes beauty hasn't gone to her head
He knows he is a man
He doesn't like to play games
He wants her more than for bed

Don't send a girl to do a woman's job
A man may have her replaced
Never send a girl to do a woman's job
A girl can't keep the pace

Dying On The Vine

Like a mellon
Without any sun
Our torrid romance
Has lost its heart

The sweetness we had
Has turned bitter
Inside our haven
If I could just remember

Our love is dying on the vine
Rapidly it withered
Love is dying on the vine
Worse than any desert

The light of our lives
Is covered with clouds
The only water produced
Comes from my eyes

Our foundation stands
On parched land
The roots of our love reach out
For survival they grasp

Our love is dying on the vine
Compassion it is without
Love is dying on the vine
Our emotions have dried out

Encore

I've wined and dined you at
The finest places around town
I took you partying
So we could really get down

In chauffeured carriages
We've seen the sights
We watched the moon
Brighten nights

What do I do for an encore
I've done everything I could
What do I do for an encore
All things under the sun

We've made love
Twelve continuous hours
Then I woke you
To champagne and flowers

Kisses and candy
Are the order of the day
Trinkets of appreciation always
Come your way

What can I do for an encore
I'm not certain
What will I do for an encore
I will keep on searching

Everything I Do Is For You

I will work eighty hours a week
With all the overtime I can get
I will never miss a call
To cherish your kiss

I will always be around
You can beep me on my beeper
I will never be too busy
To come and see you

Everything I do is for you
From the moment I awake
Everything I do is for you
It lasts all day

When day comes
I see your image
As night flows
My love is never ending

The best things in life aren't free
Your love I want to earn
If you aren't ready for me
I will wait my turn

Baby, everything I do is for you
Your love is new
Honey, everything I do is for you
You and only you

Everything Sweet Is You

Hey sweetie pie
Topped with strawberries
Cherries too
I say this, because
Everything sweet is you

You are cotton candy
Cake, honey, juice
Your love is confection
Sweetheart, everything sweet is you

You are chocolate inside
Coco outside
Rainbow groove
Symmetrically smooth
Perfectly fused
Darling, everything sweet is you

The proof is in the pudding
I love your taste
Whatever my mood
No one will ever be
Sweet as you

Exclusive Rights

I want a United States patent official
I want a certificate of bond
I want your love under lock and key
I want exclusive rights to your heart

I want you under contract
With no pictures made
You will have no personal contacts
There will be no words exchanged

I will have guards secure the property
Ready to bear arms
I will have bloodhounds on sentry
To insure exclusive rights for your love

My love for you is pure
It shines like polished armor
I will cherish you forever
To you will come no harm

You will have no secret wishes
You won't harbor any hidden clauses
I reserve the right
To be your one and only

You will not be able
To read between lines
You are the lady of my choice
I will do my own time

Our love won't be open to the public
We will perform behind closed doors
I won't display my emotions
I am in complete control

All decisions are mine
All prices I will pay
I will renew my lease
For you everyday
I want exclusive rights for your love

Face

I look into your face
To see if our love will be everlasting
Your face wanders
Is our love passing

I question your face
To know if I belong to you
Your face disguises
One plus one equals two

I want your face to declare
There is no other
Your face signifies me
As another lover

I want to rely on your face
To express our love as true
Your face says "Just us"
Is that me and you?

The concern in your face
Is it for real
Your face masks
Everything you feel

Fantastic!

Like being on the Starship Enterprise
The top of a Ferries Wheel
A view of Downtown Chicago
A rising submarine

Your love is fantastic!
One-thousand wonderful dreams
Your love is fantastic!
Better than make-believe

You make love
Like a woman possessed
You do it with such perfection
A whole lot of finesse

Like skydiving
Through the crystal blue sky
Loving you is beautiful
Fireworks on the Fourth of July

Your love is fantastic!
Better than an M.J. score
Your love is fantastic!
A round-the-world tour

With your love
No one can compete
You make love
An outstanding feat

You are fantastic!
No doubt
Your love is fantastic!
I could not love without!

Fight Fire With Love

You come to me grouchy
You have fury in your eyes
Sometimes you act so mean
You could make a witch cry

You refuse to do
Anything that I ask
You are so grumpy, if you smiled
Your face would break

I am going to fight fire with love
I will kiss and hug you
I am going to fight fire with love
It is the best remedy for you

I never hear
Laughter coming from you
Your emotions are so pent-up
You just don't know what to do

You appear frustrated
You go around half-cocked
Let me tell you one thing honey
My love is the key to your lock

I am going to fight fire with love
I will caress your anger down
I am going to fight fire with love
My love will keep you sound

Find Them, Fun Them, Forget Them

He likes party girls
He doesn't want to marry
He likes to mess around
To have a cherry

He goes to singles bars
Even the local place
He picks the one he wants
You see it on her face

First he buys her a couple rounds
Then they dance to some songs
Next they make whoopee
Like a puff of smoke, he's gone

Find them, fun them, forget them
That is his only plan
Find them, fun them, forget them
1 night stands

He doesn't want phone numbers
Or know where you work
He wants no clues
He is just a flirt

You will find him wherever there's a party
Rapping to the fast ladies
That is his routine
For some serious playing

Find them, fun them, forget them
Night time flings
Find them, fun them, forget them
That is his only dream

Flash

I'm fast as a rabbit
Going down a greased laundry chute

I'm in bed sleep
Before the light goes kaput

I'm swifter than speedy gonzales
A real shooting star

I'm a roadrunner for sure
Faster than a jaguar

My name is flash
I'm hot out the pan
I'm flash
Quicker than lightning

I move like a thoroughbred
I race like a boat

I'm fleet as an arrow
Double exposure

I propel like a jet
Accelerate like a missile

I launch like a rocket
More rapid than a whistle

I'm flash
I move at a fired pace
This is flash
I'm on my way

Flora Gold

In the park
One bright sunlit day
I see you from a distance
Hope you come my way

As we approach
Lady, you are so fine
I lose my cool
But, I come to my senses
And do what my heart tells me to

I ask your name
You say Flora Gold, sweetly
My emotions go out of bounds
You are definitely class—with style

I ask your destination
You reply; a stroll through the park
You also consent to my next question
Can I be a part

We talk and walk
As we come to know each other better
Your conversation is so down to earth
I know I am in seventh heaven

I ask for your hand
Flora Gold
I feel love untold

Flora Gold
Never bought, Never sold
Sweet, Flora Gold

We stop at the wishing well
I toss in two coins
One for me, one for you
I wish you would be mine
And I will be yours too

You confirm my desire
With one beautiful kiss
You make me feel like
My life will never be remiss

Flora Gold
You are everything a man could ask for
Plus more

Flora Gold
Love is your soul
Flora Gold

Flora Gold
When you were born
They broke the mold
Flora Gold
Your love is complete-whole
Darling, Flora Gold

Oh! Flora
Hey! Flora
Ooh! Flora
You are gold

Sweet-Flora Gold

Fool Me Once (Shame On Me)
Fool Me Twice (Shame On You)

You put me in a trick bag
Took my last dime
You were trying to get over
Half-stepping with your jive

I would have given
Anything that you asked
You took me for granted
You were moving too fast

Fool me once (Shame on me)
You think you have won
Fool me twice (Shame on you)
Not for long

Everything that goes around
Comes right back at you
Enjoy it while you can
Before it turns to disaster

When you are down and out
And looking for a friend
Remember your past
The one that you did in

Fool me once (Shame on me)
Do not try to take it easy
Fooled you twice (Shame on you)
Your road is too greasy

Friend

A friend is a person
Who is always near
When problems arise
A friend stops to hear

A friend sticks with you
No matter what
When you are down
A friend picks you up

A friend does not talk
Out of both sides the mouth
A friend does not say
I am going North
Then end South

A friend you can depend on
Night and day
A friend will not turn back
Or run away

A friend always has
A hand to lend
From start to finish
You are a friend

I value you friend

Get Involved

If you see crime happening
Call the police
Don't wait for the criminal
To beat feet

If a thief snatches
A lady's purse
Chase the hood
Don't put crime first

Get involved
Become a part of the act
Get involved
Don't stand back

Dogs bark, alarms sound
And bells ring
There is no better witness
Than us, human beings

Crime is epidemic
Around the world
Let's start by
Protecting our neighborhoods

Get involved
Blow a whistle
Get involved
Arrest this condition

Get Married: For Love

Oh! She's so pretty
Man is he fine!
But, will those traits
Last—a lifetime?

His suit is tailored
Her dress is silk
Are those good reasons
To share a quilt?

Get Married: For Love
And nothing else
Get Married: For Love
Don't second guess

Years of happiness
You will obtain
Your hearts will know
Love is no game

Walk hand in hand
Share each others dreams
Then go to the altar
When you know love is real

Get Married: For Love
Pure matrimony
Get Married: For Love
Have a joyful ceremony

Gig

The excitement has worn off
The glamour is gone
When problems become multiple
I am on my own

There is no end
To the frustration I feel
I am in a world
That is not for real

It is go, go, go
I never stop
I am constantly on the move
Like hands on a clock

I have no sense of accomplishment
I do not have hope or dreams
I sacrifice my time
For a home on wheels

The pay is not worth the tears
All the money in the world
Could not keep me here

Glamorous

You are better than pretty
Finer than fine
You're glamorous
You blow mens' minds

Men call you star
They are definitely right
To me you are more
Baby, you are out of sight

The way you move and groove
Makes men shake
Women even notice
You just leave them in your wake

You are better than pretty
Finer than fine
You're glamorous
You blow mens' minds

People know you're all class
Your words are few
They do all the talking
You're just too cool

Your heart is in the right place
You don't play around
Wherever you venture
You know the town

You are better than pretty
Top of the line
You're glamorous
Lady, you blew my mind

Goldmine

He lied
Like he couldn't do without
He takes her out
Just to show her off

When he tapped her
She put a hump in his back
That's how he spread the rumor
She put on a good act

Goldmine
His major shot
Goldmine
Tamed him no doubt

She doesn't have to lay
He will do anything she asks
With the flick of her finger
Fever rushes his head

If by chance you meet her
Don't even try to rap
Fool Man Willie
Supplies too much cash

Goldmine
Her feet never touch the ground
Goldmine
Charlie Popcorn is always around

Good Guys Finish First

It has been said before
It will be said again
You hear it on the streets
Across this land

Man meets woman
He better not treat her nice
She will get the best of him
Then take flight

I am here to tell you
I treat my lady nice
I got it from parents
Glad I took their advice

Good guys finish first
In the movies it's always last
Good guys finish first
It is not a thing of the past

I'm not worried about what people say
They are just words to me
My baby deserves the attention I give her
Our love is more than a passing fling

I'll continue to treat my lady like a queen
I know she will stay with me
I don't have any suspicions
We are happy as can be

Good guys finish first
It happens in real life
Good guys finish first
They treat ladies right

Got A Live One

She's good
Knows exactly how to move
With her
I stay in the grove

My wishes
Are all her commands
I am the one
With the master plan

Got a live one
I just reeled her in
Got a live one
I showed her good love to give

She thought she had me
It was the around the other way
She made a move
I had the ace

When she came up for air
I had my net
I didn't give her time
To second guess

Got a live one
Can't you see
Got a live one
Watch me reap

Great!

Our love is great!
From it I won't escape
Our love is great!
To sweet to be counterfeit or fake

We met not too long ago
I was convinced friendship would not score
Till our first kiss
After I walked you to your door
Lady you did not have to do anything more

Our love is great!
It could be no other way
Our love is great!
My heart is filled with you always

A player I thought I was
I was performing in the wrong field
Since we have been together
Our love makes Mount Everest look like a hill
We are closer than Jack and Jill

Our love is great!
Romance with magnificent taste
Our love is great!
With you, I always touch home plate!

Grog

It grabs hold of you
Like some raging monster
Wrestles you to the ground
Then makes you responsible

You can't fight it
There is just no win
You have got to be cool
Lest go on a binge

Grog—that's an alcoholic beverage
Grog—has all the leverage

You think you're up
When you are nothing but down
Grog steps on you
And doesn't even frown

You try to bounce back
To take a second chance
The bout is finished
Yesterday was your last

Grog—is no friend of A.A.
Grog, has no price to pay

Ground Zero

There is no winning
In nuclear confrontation
The final result
-Total annihilation

The proliferation of weapons
Stockpiled by the world
Staggers the imagination
To be used just once

Ground zero is inevitable claim
Ground zero is madness, insane

The fallout would be absolute
Life could not exist
For those who survived
Nothing would be left

Every living creature
Would rapidly expire
This planet-earth
Would be engulfed in fire

Ground zero-
We need sound organization
To stop the craziness

Handshake

Some handshakes are strong
Others are like noodles
Some are limp
The kind that doodle

A handshake represents
The person you meet
You can feel a winner
Or one to defeat

Oh, you claim arthritis
Don't use an excuse
If you like me
Don't be aloof

Don't nod
Or try to wink
With those gestures
I'll know you are a fink

Grab my hand
Pump it hard
You are an adult
It is in your heart

Have You Hugged Your Child Today

He has been to school
Had a hard day
He wanted to confide in his classmates
Who looked the other way

He doesn't feel like playing
Stays locked in his room
He won't eat his dinner
He refuses to watch cartoons

Have you hugged your child today
Showed him that you care
Have you hugged your child today
Told him that your life is his to share

Have you hugged your child today
Given him lots of affection
Have you hugged your child today
Tried to resolve his rejection

Children are little people
They have feelings too
Ups and downs
With rainbow colored moods

They need help to grow up
Become a woman or man
For right now
They just want you to understand

Have you hugged your child today
Told him you will guide his way
Have you hugged your child today
Told him tomorrow will be a better day

Have you hugged your child today
Let him express his views
Have you hugged your child today?
Do it!

Here Come The Tears

You left me, baby
I have not gotten over you yet
My broken heart
Makes it impossible . . .
For me to forget

You are on my mind, darling
Twenty-four hours everyday
Your love was too great
Just to go away

Here come the tears
Rolling down my face
Here come the tears
Our home is an empty space

When I awake
Honey, I feel your presence near
Reality takes over
My thoughts turn to despair

At that exact second
A swelling starts in my eyes
I hold my head down
That is when I begin to cry

Here come the tears
My clothes are soaking wet
Here come the tears
Sweetheart: You—I will never forget

Heres Looking At You Kid

We look each other in the eyes
As we toast our love,
Celebrate our happiness
Champagne—for all our good

Glasses clink
Expressing our vibes
The candlelight setting
Accents the time

Heres looking at you kid
Eye to eye
Heres looking at you kid
Smile to smile

My lady
We have travelled from afar
Ah, Casablanca
By way of Key Largo

What do you say sweetheart
Let's do it again
With our special song—
Play it again Sam

Heres looking at you kid
Don't stop
Heres looking at you kid
To the top

Hit The Ground Running

I was really getting down
When I heard a key in the door
She belonged to another
We were on the second stroke

I grabbed my wallet
Headed straight for the window
There was only one way out
He was blocking that entrance

I hit the ground running
Streaking like a bat
I hit the ground running
And I never looked back

I heard a couple of rounds
Take off in the air
Tears formed an X
Behind my head

I was moving so fast
You could put a checkerboard on my back
My feet were doing a hundred
It was no act

I kissed the ground running
Wishing nothing gained
I hit the ground flying
And I wasn't ashamed

Hold A Candle

I want to hold a candle
Close to you love
To show you
How much you mean to me

I want to hold a candle
Near you—my heart
To glow, for how truly happy
You have made me

I want to hold a candle
Next to you lady
Let it shine through the night

I want to hold a candle
Right by you darling
While I squeeze you tight

My candle will illuminate you
It will accent your day
It will burn twenty-four hours
For your loving ways

My candle will glow
Like a rocket in the sky
It will burn brilliantly
Display your sensuous vibes

I want to hold a candle
To you, sweet one
Tell you: "You are my only love"

I want to hold a candle
Beside you, my love, while
I cuddle you with kisses and hugs

I want to hold a candle
For you my love
Because you treat me like a king
You are my queen

I am want to raise a candle
For you my love
You have exceeded all of
My wishes and dreams
You love is from above

Hold It Right There

I was getting down with my lady
We were having a good time
She told me I was not doing it right
That is where I drew the line

I grabbed her by the ankles
Put her in a buck
She told me to work faster
Gold I had struck

She said: "Hold it right there daddy!"
I said: "Is it good, is it good?"
She said: "Honey don't move!"
I said: "Baby I should"
She said: "Hurt me daddy!"
I knew I could

Her eyes got glassy
As she took me in
She hit a tremendous peak
While I wore myself thin

I tried to out do myself
There was nothing left
We had worked ourselfs into a frenzy
We both lost our breath

She said: "Hold it right there daddy!"
I said: "Was it good, was it good?"
She said: "Baby don't move!"
I said: "I wish I could!"
She said: "Hurt me baby!"
I said: "Are you sure?"

Hot And Cold

Sometimes we make love and it's
Really out of sight
Other times we lay
I can't touch you all night

When we kiss
You make my lips sizzle
Then in the next moment
I can't get a nibble

You run hot and cold
Like electricity from a socket
Hot and cold
Like water from a faucet

Somedays you are total passion
And you don't want me to go away
Then other times
You just let the flame fade

Sometimes I hold your hand and
Feel a flaming pulsation
But in a short while
Your feelings are fluctuating

Baby, you run hot and cold
Just like winter's ire
Hot and cold
You are ice and fire

How Could I Not Love You

You are beautiful, so pretty
But you seem to have self-doubt
You are pleasing and charming
Yet confidence you are without

With your credentials
You should be a queen
I would place flowers at your feet
And apply to be your king

How could I not love you
As sweet as you are
How could I not love you
You will be my shining star

You seem so reclusive
You say no one will go out with you
You are apprehensive about talking
Afraid that your message
Will not get through

You are a real life Cinderella
With no pumpkin in sight
I want to be the man
Who will see you through the night

How could I not love you
You are more than I could wish for
How could I not love you
Just let me hold you in my arms

How Do You Change The System?

How do you change the system

Do you shoot it with a gun
Do you cut it with a knife
Do you ignore the president
Or not follow his wife

Do you start a revolution
Do you drop a bomb
Do you smuggle in weapons
And pull a coup de grace

Do you work from within
As some type of cancer
And hope that the results
Will become everlasting

Do you demolish it for the better
For the sake of future generations
So that we may live
Without social degradation

Finally,
Do you pray
For the liberation of our people
One day?

Myles W. Wallace

How Do You Know You're In Love?

The air breathes fresh and clean
Everything is new
You walk tall off the ground
All is just for two

Everything is wonderful
Life is grand
Nature is spontaneous
There is no need to plan

How do you know you're in love?
The day starts to rise
How do you know you're in love?
Nights move you higher

There are never disagreements
Peace is at hand
You've become each best friend
You are the other's greatest fan

Life knows no disappointments
Positive attitudes for each other
A total one=on-one relationship
Never to be shared by another

How do you know you're in love?
Happy—the bottom line
How do you know you're in love?
Life is fine!

I Am Vulnerable To Your Love

Like a magnet
You draw me near
Control my desires
Soothe my fear

You overwhelm me with charm
Temper me with your beauty
You keep me motivated
With your winning ingenuity

Superman has a weakness
Krypton is it
I am only human
Your love I cannot quit

My heart you have captured
I am sensitive to your touch
You overpower my mind
Loving you, I cannot get enough

I am thrilled by your thoughtful wishes
Stimulated with your fruitful kisses
I gravitate to submission
Feeling euphoric
Buoyed by my condition

Frosted phrases only give hint
How much I am in love with you
I am vulnerable to your love
I have to have you near
Hold you close
To whisper sweet words
Gently in your ear

You lure me with delicious food
Attract me with stylish dress
Tempt me with tantalizing treats
You are at ease
Being the best

Your irresistible personality
Keeps my heart in check
I have no plans to leave
I am totally yours
There is no reason to suspect

Stay pretty, darling
My heart you melt
Complete woman
Your love is more than wealth

Gorgeous, I am vulnerable to your love
Your grace claimed me whole
I am your man
Baby, keep me on

I Am Your Man

I am you man
Let me lead the way
Take my hand
Today is an all new day

No use waiting in line
Men stand back!
I love this lady
This is no act

I am your man, sweetheart
Baby, don't you know
I am your man
You are the star in our show

No one will ever take your place
You will always be tops
That is the bottom line
My love you cannot stop

We were made for each other
I am your lighthouse of love
The love I have for you
Is guided from above

Darling, I am your man
Our love is so sweet
You are my world
You made my life complete

I Confess

Darling, I confess that I love you
This you already know
I can't hold back any longer
My love continues to grow

Honey, I confess that I care
You mean the world to me
You are always on my mind
My life is complete

Sweetheart, I confess that I love you
I don't have to go to court
My love is supreme
You are my choice

Sugar, I confess that I adore you
This poem is my testimony
I want to be sentenced
To a lifetime of matrimony

Dearest, I confess—I need you
Don't ever go away
Without you in my heart
I could not make the day

I Cried In My Dream

I was so lonely
You left me this weekend
Our love trilogy
Became my anthology
Since we would not be together again

I went to bed Sunday morning
After staying up Saturday night
I fell into a deep sleep immediately
Right away I was dreaming
I could see your face very explicitly

You were in another mans' arms
Because of my alleged non-attention
He was holding you tight
You were not resisting
Kiss me you were insisting

I cried in my dream
It was so for real
I cried in my dream
Tears I did not conceal

He whispered sweet nothings in your ear
Expressions that made me toss and turn
I felt as if I were in a thunderstorm
I hollered out loud
My heart began to burn

I cried in my dream
Darling, hear my plea
I cried in my dream
Will you come back to me?

I woke up the next morning
My clothes were all wet
Darling, come on home
I will keep you satisfied
This is where you belong

I Didn't Realize How Much I Loved You—Until You Left

I took your love for granted
Not knowing the price I would pay
You knew that day was coming
When you left me this way

You were so good to me
Do anything that I asked
Somehow I neglected you
Our love became a thing of the past

I didn't realize how much I loved you
Until the day you left
I didn't realize how much I loved you
Surely you jest

You've been gone only since yesterday
The tears keep on flowing
If I could rearrange things over the years
Our love would be a winner scoring

I want to be with you, if just once again
Make up for all the lost time
I can never get enough of your sweet love
You bring pure joy into this life of mine

I didn't realize how much I loved you
Words could never describe
I didn't realize how much I loved you
Your love will always be my pride

I Didn't Want To Make Love To You The First Time—Version Two

I didn't want to make love to you the first night
I wanted to savor that hour last
I didn't want to make love to you the first night
Our love, I didn't want in the past

I walked you to my door
I didn't want you to leave
You looked so good standing there
Oh yeah, Cleopatra in blue jeans

Just for a second
I wanted you to stay
The thought of you being here
I had to let you go away

I didn't want to make love to you the first night
I sure had the desire to
I didn't want to make love to you the first night
Our love, I wanted to be true

Our bodies were close
Tenderly they touched
If I made love to you the first night
Love would not have been long enough

Our eyes met
As we held each other tight
Embraced together
I wanted to hold you all night

I didn't want to make love to you the first night
I wanted our love to care for
I didn't want to make love to you the first night
Our love, I want to last forever

I Do Need You

I don't need sun
To make the day bright
I do need you
You are the sunshine
That makes my life bright

I don't need stars
To shine in the night
I do need you
You are the stars
My light in the night

I don't need rain
That makes flowers grow
I do need you
You are the water
Which lets my heart grow

I don't need wind
Which cultivates this land
I do need you
You blow my mind
You are the only one for me
In this land

I Don't Go There

My woman and I had made love
In just about every position possible
When she told me
"Honey! I want to try something new!
Let's do something different!"
She wanted me to go down
To savor the fuzzy fountain
To me, that was mission impossible

She was real persistent, when she told me
Sampling would put her in ecstasy
She said: "I will guide you there,
Darling please be patient"

I got about half the way
The thought of bringing her off
Would have made my day
But I didn't have the nerve
To go the rest of the way

I looked my lady straight in her
Wide and pretty brown eyes
I said, baby: "I don't go there"
She stared at me passionately, and said
"Darling, don't you even care?"

We made love
Throughout the night and most of
The next day
When my lady whispered:
"I want you to *really* please me daddy
Take me to the mountain-clear"
I said: "Sweetheart, I don't go there!"

Myles W. Wallace

Tears fell from her face
I changed my heart
As she began to part . . . .

Friends always ask me
When was the last time "I took a dare"
My answer is always the same
Don't bet any money
Because, brother, I don't go there

I Know It When I See It

I don't know how to describe it
I can't tell you how it looks
It could be in a picture
Or outside of a book

Deep throat contained it
Behind the green door
Check it out on the streets
Or inside a room-cloaked

I know it when I see it
I'm talking about pornography
I know it when I see it
Weird photography

It's disguised in movies
How about eight pages
You'll find it in peep shows
Expressed by its' players

You receive it in the mail
It is fourth class
You can search for it
At your local newsstand

I know it when I see it
It smacks me like pie
I'm talking about pornography
I know it when I see it
I cannot tell a lie

I Love You, Darling

I love you, darling
Beautiful honey
I love you sugar
You lovely woman

It's not the way you style your hair
Or clothes you wear so neat
It's the way you freshen the air
And make everything near you, blossom sweet

It's not the way you walk or talk
That makes you look so nice
It's the way you use your words
How you fashion your lips
That makes me look twice

I love you, darling
Pretty baby
I adore you, darling
You sensuous lady

It's not your youth that attracts me
Nor is it your pretty smile that excites me
It's how you know what being a lady means
Your view is from the top
You are in all of my dreams

It's not your education that turns me on
Or your beautiful personality
That keeps me coming back
It's how you use your charm
To get to where you belong
You have my heart
My mind won't take long

I love you, darling
Candy sweet
I love you baby
You're wonderful—complete

I Need A Woman

I don't need a girl
Who can't make up her mind
I don't need a girl
Who likes to whine

I need a woman
That knows where to go
I need a woman
To star in her show

I don't need a girl
Who can't make decisions
I don't need a girl
That has no vision

I need a woman
Who uses knowledge to advance
I need a woman
Who has the masters' plan

I don't want a girl
That likes to run and hide
I don't need a girl
Who won't stand by my side

I need a woman
To be with me, thick or thin
I need a woman
Who plays to win

Darling, I need a woman
Come home honey

I Think Not

Do I want to leave
Run away—hide
Be by myself
With only time
At my side

Do I want to act a fool
So that you can go
And I would occupy
A empty house
All alone

I think not
It was a long shot
I think not
I would say—stop

With you is
Where I want to stay
I want your heart
I need you always

The thought happened to
Scarcely enter my mind
Immediately it was gone
I knew it was a lie

I think not
Positively
I think not
Most definitely

I Want To Deserve Your Love

Baby, when I'm cranky
Keep away from me
Sugar, if I'm ornery
Just leave me be

I'm not the easiest person
To get along with
It will be difficult
Since together we're living

Bear with me, sweetheart
I will make everything right
The most important thing is
You stay by my side

I want to deserve your love
Honey, you're sweet and good
I want to deserve your love
I have misunderstood

It won't be an easy transition
Sharing our lives
I will do my best
I will try

I won't use excuses
Have faith in me
If I am not successful
Set me—free

I want to deserve your love
Soon I will
I want to deserve your love
Darling, stay with me till then

I Want To Love You For A Lifetime

I don't want a one night affair
A one shot deal
I want to love you for a lifetime
With love that is real

I don't want love, here today
Then gone tomorrow
I want to love you endlessly
Without pain or sorrow

I don't want, wham, bam, thank you ma'am
All that type of stuff
If I loved you forever
I could never love you enough

I don't want a handshake
A peck on the cheek
I want to hold, squeeze, caress you
To love you comes with ease

I don't want to hear talk
Call me and let's be friends
The love I have for you
Will last a lifetime's end

I Want To Make Love To You Everyday

I'm gone all week
Working five to five
When I come home on the weekends
I'm kind of tired

But, I don't want to sleep
I don't even want to lie down
All want to do is make love to you
Twenty-four times—the clock goes round

Even though I'm not home
To fulfill your requests
Goodness knows—in my heart
I'm trying to do my best

One minute of your love
Indeed it would be sweet
Even with one hour
My life would only be 75 % complete

It wouldn't be a roll in the hay
I want to make love to you everyday

Weekends come and weeks pass by
Fifty-two weeks make a year
But with your love
Any day is nice to have you near

You are so fine, baby
I want to make love to you everyday

I Want To Make Love With You (Not To You)

Together as one is
How we belong
Pulsating in unison and
Never apart

However we are positioned
I will be totally yours
Our jubilant involvement
Will be shared by both

I want to make love with you
(Not to you)
This special time will be only ours

I am going to make love with you
(Not to you)
These will be our greatest hours

Our bodies will blend and
Minds will combine
Inside of you
We will climax many times

We will shower in intimacy
Bath with sensuality
For the cleansing of our hearts
And healthiness of our lives

I want to make love with you
(Not to you)
To remain at our peak

I want to make love with you
(Not to you)
Darling, just you and me

I Want You

I don't want a million dollars
I don't want a Cadillac
I don't want a house on the hill
I want you baby
No fiction, just fact

I want you
Like one and one becomes two
I want you
I want you to want me too

I want you so good
You are a sweet taste in my mouth
I want you sweetheart
You're the key for my lock

I don't need a diamond ring
I don't need a rolex watch
I don't need a long mink coat
I need you honey
I love you a lot

I Wish It Were Me

Sweet kisses—Hugs
All that is love
I wish it were me

Private talks, Walks
What love is about
I wish it were me

Quiet moments, Devotion
Sharing emotions
I wish it were me

Sun shining—Light
Lives are bright
I wish it were me

Lady, Beautiful Baby
I wish it were me
It use to be

Ice

Ice for skating
Ice for drinks
Ice for hands
Ice to think

Ice from the sky
Ice in shows
Ice for necks
Ice on windows

Ice is frozen oxygen
Ice is part water

Ice is used
To do lots of things
For sliding and
Pinky rings

Ice is clear or smoked
It doesn't come cheap
You can buy it
For the times you need

Ice is slippery stuff
Ice, sensitive and rough

Myles W. Wallace

If I Were In Love

You—I kind of like
I mean I really dig
Something holds me back
One-hundred percent to give

I don't call like I should
I hardly speak your name
I never write
For your heart to claim

I can't say why
This dilemma exists
I do know one thing
For your mind, I will persist

If I were in love
The right way romance would be
If I were in love
Life we would share between

This burden alone
I don't want to carry
I reach out for your help
To make our journey easy
And bridge this barrier

Show me a little affection
Let me see your smile
How about a card or note
Just once in a while

If I were in love
We would be one
If we were in love
Emotions would never confront

If The Criminals Don't Get You, The Hoodlums Will

It's getting to the point
You can't go out on weekends
To have fun anymore
There's always someone out there
Ready to settle the score

When you do go out
For a night on the town
After you finish
Your ride may be missing
Nowhere to be found

If the criminals don't get you
The hoodlums will
Don't take any chances
You might come up missing
In a valley or hills

Sometimes you stop at the local bar
For a nice, cool drink
When you finish
Some dude wants to
Push you to the brink

The evening is done
You are heading home
The hoodlums force you over
Try to run you off the road

If the criminals don't get you
The hoodlums will
Just take life
One day at a time
Don't forget who pays the bills

Myles W. Wallace

If You Had Only Told Me

Why did you have to wait till
My love had grown strong
When there was no such thing
As turning back
When I was too far gone

My heart was bound
You never hinted, for me to know
That our love was over
And we couldn't be together anymore

The news hit me
Like a slap in the face
I was truly brokenhearted
And feel that I have been disgraced

You tell me there is another man
I can hardly stand
And to make matters worse
You said that ours' was never a romance

If you had only told me
Right from the beginning
My love I would have reconsidered
Without going to the limit

If you had only told me
I would have drawn the line
Oh, what's the use
I am so in love with you
You can have my love anytime

I'm Gonna Funk You Up

Why are you standing there
Acting so cold
I going to put you in the groove
Because I am bold

When I ask you for a dance
I don't want you to resist
I will hold your arm
If you really insist

I'm gonna funk you up
Don't you stand fast
I'm gonna funk you up
You will have funk up the aft

I'm not going to wine and dine you
All hours of the night
I'm going to do it to you
Until just before daylight

I'm not going through any changes
No more than you knew
I'm going to whoop it on you
Till it feels like brand new

I'm gonna funk you up
You have got nothing to lose
I'm gonna funk you up
Then you will be cool

Myles W. Wallace

I'm In Love Again—Not You, But Me

Somehow, along the way
I became disinterested in myself
I don't know how it happened
I don't know when I got there

A lack of self-confidence
Can come from troubled nerves
Coupled with insecurity
Makes a man reserved

It was not a situation of picking up pieces
To start over again
What really mattered
Is to know where my head is

I won't let the bottom drop out
Because, I'm in love again—not you, but me
This time I will stay on top
For the reason I'm in love again—not you, but me

Sometimes I felt up, others times down
I could not find satisfaction
I have now acquired a happy median
For myself I take time

I'm in love again—not you, but me
The world is a better place
I'm in love again—not you, but me
See the smile on my face

Immunized

No feeling you have
When it comes to a man
You were misled
By another's unfaithful plans

The theory you have about men
Is shot full of holes
The affairs you've tried to run
Went out of your control

You're immunized
Against life in general
Immunized
Just like a hospital

With your sterile mind
You block all masculine faces
Being unidentified
Becomes realization

Your feelings you've inoculated
The brain is numb
Your heart is vaccinated
For the love bug

You're immunized
A walking mannequin
Immunized
You should be in a picture window

Myles W. Wallace

Infinitely

How many ways do I love you?
Let me count the ways:

I love you more than
Stars in the sky
I love you more than
Celebrations of the Fourth of July

I love you infinitely

I love you more than
The universe has time
I love you more than
The sun will shine

I love you infinitely

I love you more than
The moon will glow
I love you more than
Summer melts snow

I love you infinitely

I love you more than
A rainbow flows
I love you more than
All the worlds' gold

Darling, I love you infinitely

Is There A Doctor In The House

My baby left me
I home all by myself
She went away weeks ago
And I haven't gotten better yet

She is always on my mind and
I don't know how to get her off
But I do know one thing for sure
Without her, I am a total loss

If she would just call
Is there a doctor in the house
She is my all
Is there a doctor in the house

I could check myself into a hospital
But I know she is my only cure
Even if I was an outpatient
She would be my medicine for sure

My world is shattered
I will never be the same
If she would only return
To relieve my pain

I will wait for her knock
Is there a doctor in the house
You see, my time is running out
Is there a doctor in the house

115

It Comes From Within

You say my love is superficial
I don't like to kiss or touch
I never show emotion
And we don't make love enough

You tell me my thoughts are elsewhere
I don't concentrate on you
I won't say sweet little things
I'm always so blue

When I call you on the phone
My conversation is too short
If I write you a letter
The text is erroneous

You say I won't buy you a diamond ring
Pretty clothes or expensive gifts
Sugar, just let me say this;

I do love you, sincere
Every emotion that I feel
Comes from within

I always think of you
Like my heart beats
I have visions of you
Soft, beautiful, sweet

My arms yearn to embrace you
To make my life complete
My mind craves just for you
You are the very breath of me

Don't you ever think
I just don't care
Like earth rings the sun
My love comes from within

It Will Never Be Over For You And Me

You say no more you love me
Don't look your way
Don't write any letters
Don't even call your name

We had terrific times together
We were never apart
Now that you're not around
Pain fills my heart

I'm an optimist
I'll never give up
No matter what you say
I love you more than much

Baby, It will never be over for you and me
Memories too sweet
Inside me, you'll always be
Baby, It will never be over for you and me

I won't use the excuse
I'm only human
Subject to mistakes
To be with you
I'll do whatever it takes

If there is another
Attempting to take my place
Believe me, it won't happen
I have abundant faith

Baby, It will never be over for you and me
You make my life complete
You're lady elite
Can't you see, honey
Darling, it will never be over for you and me

Myles W. Wallace

Give love a chance
To guide our way
Let's start right now
For brighter days

Sugar, It will never be over for you and me
You're all the woman I need
My heart reveals, love I can't conceal
Baby, It will never be over for you and me

I've Become In Love With You

Like a pickle becomes a cucumber
A raisin ripens to a prune
Winter changes to summer
May turns to June
I've become in love with you

A caterpillar becomes a butterfly
Night develops to day
Dough bakes to bread
Work is exchanged for pay
I've become in love with you

A girl blossoms to woman
Sand revolves to glass
A boy grows to man
Dreams materialize to plans
I've become in love with you

Time is transformed to a clock
A mountain renders rocks
Cities are built from blocks
I went from bottom to top
I've become in love with you

I've Got Something I Want To Tell The World (I Love You)

I could shout it from a house top
Or print it in the daily press
If I used a bullhorn
That would be better yet

I could get on the telephone
Perhaps the Internet
I'll send my message ship to shore
I'll say it whatever way is best

I've got something I want to tell the world
I love you

I've got something I want to tell the world
No one, I place above you

I'll spread my news across the sky
With the help of a G.E. Blimp
For what I have to say
No letter will they miss

I want to put my tidings in a rocketship
Send it into outerspace
I want the universe to know
Only you occupy my heart—my special place

I've got something I want to tell the world
I love you

I've got something I want to tell the world
All the galaxies too

We will walk together
Hand in hand
Our love for each other will be
Better than the promised land

No earthly force
Could ever tear us apart
Our bond will last forever
Longer than all the stars

I've got something I want to tell the world
I love you

I've got something I want to tell the world
I love you
You and only you

Jesse Can Win

Critics said he didn't have
A snowball's chance of winning
The Presidential Election
Back in 1984 . . . .
Jesse went out and campaigned
And won millions of votes

Jesse—the emancipator
Truly opened the presidential door
He is more than qualified
To run the 1997 show

That is all the more reason
People should know
We have to get out—vote
Vote, vote and vote

Jesse can win
Jesse can win
Say it loud
Jesse can win
Jesse can win
Say it proud

As we approach this century's turn
This country is long overdue for change
Jesse is the man
No doubt about it
With something to say
Intelligent and sane

On Election Day, whether you vote absentee
Pull a lever or punch a card
At all times
Especially, while you stand in line
Keep Jesse on your mind

Jesse is a mediator
Definitely a negotiator
He has never been a procrastinator
Or deviator
Truly he is an innovator

Jesse can win
Jesse can win
Jesse can win

All the people have to do is register
Then go out and vote, vote and vote

Jesse is the man!
Jesse has the plan!
Jesse stands for equality
On all lands!

Jesse needs a chance
Just like we have given others
He has earned the civil right
The man is a winner!
Jesse Jackson knows how to govern!

Jesse can win
Jesse can win
People—just vote
Go out and vote and vote and vote
Jesse can win
Jesse can win
Make the cynics take note

Jesse can win!
Jesse can win!
All we have to do is vote!
Jesse will win!
Jesse will win!
Don't let the critics boast!

Jesse will win!
Jesse will win!
Now get out there and vote!

Kiss Me Gently

Above the moonlit crystal lake
My sweetheart and I stand on
The twilight terrace
Scintillating scents sensitize the air
The world is in cinematic view
Truly it is time for sharing

Regal doves play a serenade
In the breeze
Royal flowers sway softly in tempo
Love's melody is syncopated
It is tender times like this
That make life so soothingly uncomplicated

In the harbor, near the coast
An empty boat has broken its mooring
The craft is drifting out of port
Suddenly it reverses direction
In a futile attempt to
Return to shore

On this warm most memorable night
I pull my lady close to me
In that same moment, we look up
Thank our lucky star
As our lips touch ever so gingerly

Kiss me gently
Kiss me gently
As waves nudge the boat
Kiss me gently, darling
Soft, like water lilies float

The boat sits idle
With nowhere to go
Water splashes its sides
The captain's door becomes ajar
Then the vessel rocks and fro

We break our embrace
To observe the boat's erie mystic plight
I hold my lady's hand
We ponder, if our kiss
Was wrong or right

In the distance on a clearing
There is a man with some type of harness
He is heading toward the yacht of lost bearings
Approaching the boat
He lashes out the rope
In a valiant attempt to snare it

He misses his first try
Immediately he lets the rope fly again
Success is his this time
A smile etches his face
When he reels the boat in

I squeeze my loves hand
In one motion
We are very close—together
I say to my lady

Kiss me gently
Kiss me gently
To part—never

Kiss me gently
Kiss me gently
I hold her tightly
I know everything is fine
With her—life is always exceedingly better

Kiss me gently
As the moon pecks
Diamond sand crystals

Kiss me gently
Baby, kiss me gently
Like the current flows
Up river—so magnificently

Ladies Of The Night

Ladies of the night
Men have no fear
Ladies of the night have existed
Since the world has been here

See them strolling
Down and up the street
You can place a call and
A location they will meet

They are out to make living
Just like everyone else
Beside that, it is the worlds'
Oldest profession

Don't go out
And call them names
To you
They will never bring shame

Ladies of the night
Keep doing your trade
Without you, the world
Would not have been made

Let Me Feel Your Love

You tell me you love me
You agree with most things I say
You call it getting to know one
My heart sees it a different way

You speak sweet words
But they have only tiny meanings
Without your love
As a man I am depleted

If you would just reach out
You have enveloped me with your charm
If you could just—open your mind
So that I may embrace your love

Let me understand it
Let me hold it
Let me touch it
Let me caress it

Let me feel your love
Without it, I numb to my soul
Let me feel your love
My emotions have lost control

Being with you
Could be the sunlight of my day
If rays of warmth
Were directed my way

You cloud your love
With an ominous haze
If I could jut break through
Convince you—I need

Myles W. Wallace

Let me taste it
Let me bathe in it
Let me live it

Let me feel your love
I will wear it
As a coat of pride
Let me feel your love
I will cherish it forever—inside

Let Them Eat Cake

No jobs they have
Extended unemployment lines
Their families can't go far
The system says all is fine

It's the depression
All over again
A recession it has been
Since their lives began

Let them eat cake
It's better than flour
Let them eat cake
Say those in power

They try every minute
To get their lives together
It adds up to-
The last day of never

Let them eat cake
It may be their last serving
Let them eat cake
They are most deserving

Like Or Love

When you like someone
You take it for granted
When you love someone
You won't take advantage

When you like a person
You don't feel it in your heart
Loving someone
That person becomes a part

Do you like or love
You are the one with the answer
Like or love
Only one is lasting

If you like someone
You play a game
To love someone is
A feeling of fame

If you like someone
They are barely on your mind
When you love someone
You think of them all the time

Like or love
Which do you prefer
Like or love
Only one is sure

Loneliness (You're A Friend No More)

In a cold room I sat
Empty beer cans surrounded me
The window shades were tightly drawn
Darkness lurked persistently

I was afraid to move
I was terrified beyond reason
Courage I could not build up
There was nothing but indecision

Indecision gripped me like vise
It held me unyieldingly
No one I could turn to and
Expose my feelings

Although we hadn't know each other long
I felt something, right from the start
With lingering desire
You—I wanted to be a part

When the telephone rang
I answered to hear your sweet voice
Off the floor I rose
To be your only choice

Loneliness (you're a friend no more)
Not since my baby
Loneliness (you're a friend no more)
We will keep you away together

Sunlight now shines in my home
From your glowing heart
My door is always open so that I can
Greet you with waiting arms

I will continuously serenade you
With flowers and candlelight
You changed my way of living
You gave me a better life

Your kind of loving
Has to be the master's plan
We reached the plateau of love
Without you, I would not have attained
Success, no doubt, is yours to claim

Loneliness (you're a friend no more)
Your time has come and gone
Loneliness (a friend no more)
To the past you belong

Look Deeper Than Eyes Can See

I have on a shirt and tie
With a three piece suit
Every month I pay rent
Materialism is proof

Under these clothes is a person
With a heart that beats
I like to have a good time
With one who has feelings

Look deeper than eyes can see
Farther than money
Look deeper than eyes can see
Life is sunny

First impressions
Can go either way
Don't jump to conclusions
Better to investigate

We have a lot in common
We are both human beings
We live in the same world
And share all things

Look deeper than eyes can see
Not the words I speak
Look deeper than eyes can see
See me for me

Myles W. Wallace

Losing You

It is like a bird saying
I am scared of heights
Or; "I don't like silk"
Says the spider

A thunderstorm
In the sky blue
Or sand blowing
Against the mountain view

Losing you—inconceivable
Losing you—unbelievable

The sun not shining
Above the clouds
Trees shrinking
Over the ground

A weight lifter
Without any muscles
Or the bride to be
Saying she is uncertain

Losing you—unconventional
Losing you—reprehensible

Love

I see birds serenading air
Flowers blooming everywhere
Truly it is a time to share

I feel love

I see couples holding hands
Joy between woman and man
Compassion across this land

I feel love

I see shining sunlight
The high moon bright
Stars showering night
Sparkle in my life

I feel love

I cherish the tenderness of your kiss
The sweetness of your lips
Love has me convinced
Life is bliss

I feel love

Love Hit Me Like A Rock (Doe Dum)

I woke up one morning
Feeling real good
I had been with a fine lady
Man, she was good

I went to work
She was constantly on my mind
I couldn't do my job
Thinking of her all the time

Love hit me like a rock (Doe Dum)
Yeah, just that quick
Love hit me like a rock (Doe Dum)
By the love bug I had been bit

Everytime I look up
I am dialing her number
Was I rational
I began to wonder

No matter where I go
Or what I do
She is with me
Exclusive

Love hit me like a rock (Doe Dum)
Hey, just like cannon shot
Love hit me like a rock (Doe Dum)
I can't stop

Love Seeks Its On Level

Sometimes it is meant for lovers
To be no more than friends
Other times sweethearts can carry
Love to the very end

There will come a time when
Love has gone as far as it can
It is difficult to understand
Where you have never been

You see, love seeks its on level
Like a river ready to crest
Take love one day at a time
Step by step
While you second guess

Love was meant for everyone
Love just comes in different ways
Love is joyful, yet mysterious
Love always has the last say

When you get that overpowering feeling
Every situation seems great
Take a second look at love
You may want to escape

Because love seeks its own level
Like a basin overfilled
At times it is high
Sometimes it hits low
You have to learn
How to go with the flow

Myles W. Wallace

Madman About Your Love

When it comes to your love
I'm Dr. Jekyll, Mr. Hyde
Frankenstein, Jack The Ripper
And The Incredible Dr. Phibes

I'm Wolfman
Dracula—Boo!
Bigfoot, Wolfman
Svenghoula—too

I'm a madman about your love
Girl I'll eat you up
I'm a madman about your love
For you I'm strong and tough

I'll jump off buildings
Kick down doors
I will peer through windows
Pace the floor

No obstacle is too great
To keep me from you
Your love is so hot
No way I can be cool

I'm a madman about your love
Delirious as a loon
I'm a madman about your love
Crazy like a goon

Mama Hayga's Children

Be ye light or dark
I don't care what color you are

We are Mama Hayga's children

Moms and Dads alike
You are Mama Hayga's tykes

Mama Hayga goes back a long, long way
To the times when three ships
Made it across the Atlantic
To the Plymouth Bay

She is the mother of all folks
Including those who call themselves heroes

Mama Hayga goes back a long way
Back to when people were slaves
She cared for the sick
She helped the old
Mama Hayga had a whole lot of soul

She was there in all the wars
Making sure soldiers met no harm

Mama Hayga didn't go to school
Her school was the golden rule

"Do unto to others
As you would have them do unto you
Just do it to them
Before they do it to you"

From cotton fields to floods
Mama Hayga's cry could be heard

"Praise the Lord in these times and conditions
Hurry up and pass the doggone ammunition"

From mellon fields to civil rights fronts
Mama Hayga was sometimes zonked

But somehow she maintained her cool
Telling people: "I ain't nobody's fool"

Mama Hayga was something else alright
It was best to take her advice

"Do unto others
As you would have them do unto you
Just don't get yourself over a barrel
And let them do it to you"

Mans'—Inhumanity To—Man

Mans'—inhumanity to—man
War is the major form
Of this disgusting trait
Crime is another part
In this malicious wave

Add pushers to the list
Who peddle dope for profit
And gang members
Who demand your wallet

Mans'—inhumanity to—man
Why can't we control
Mans'—inhumanity to—man
Insanity continues to unfold

Discrimination surely is
Another artery of aggression
Denial of education
Fuels this desperate situation

Linked with prisoners
Who don't recognize right
And the handicapped without access
To their right to life

Mans'—inhumanity to—man
We must shoulder the blame
Mans'—inhumanity to—man
Bear the shame

Marilyn Belonged To No One

She was a beautiful woman
Every man wish
She was so much woman
So voluptuous

The way she shimmied when she walked
Men lost their minds
They tried to buy her
She was just that fine

Marilyn belonged to no one
Only to herself
Marilyn belonged to no one
To no one else

She had tons of charisma
An abundance of charm
She led a mystic life
A glamorous one

Somewhere—beyond
She still exists
She remains an enigma
—Intricate

Marilyn belonged to no one
Only to the stars
Marilyn belonged to no one
Now she is a part

Meet Me At The Airport, Baby

You could meet me at the bus station
That would be too slow
You could watch me ride in
The old train depot

I want to see you
Just as soon as I can
I can hardly wait
For this plane to land

Meet me at the airport, baby
I want to see you so bad
Meet me at the airport, baby
Where I'll hold you fast

I would walk a hundred miles
Think of you every step
Or sail a boat
My message would be S.O.S.

If I decided to ski
Cross the mountains high
My love would reach out
Touch the sky

Meet me at the airport, darling
To each other we'll belong
Meet me at the airport, baby
I'm coming home

My Feet Got The Beat

The D.J. was jamming
But no one was getting up
To get down
There didn't seem to be
A dancer
Anywhere in the crowd

Then the D.J. played
This record called 'The Game'
It was an instant hit
His claim to fame

My feet got the beat
Man, I started partying
My feet got the beat
I partied hearty

The rhythm of the song
Was real tight
That bass was thumping
To dancers delight

The lyrics were perfect
They had verve
The crowd moved in time
With every word

My feet got the beat
People were dancing
Everywhere I could see

My feet got the beat
That night
I partied complete

My Ghetto Mansion

It is not on a mountaintop
Nor is it on a hill
It is not in a valley
But it is my home still

I do not live on
A tree lined street
And there is no garden of roses
Beneath my feet

My ghetto mansion
Is filled with love
My ghetto mansion
Is a house that is a home

I do not have a butler
A chauffeur I do not need
A maid is not in line
Because, I will fix myself a spot-of-tea

I paint and fix-up
Designers I will not have
Love graces my home
It shines like a chandelier

My ghetto mansion
Is a place that gives
My ghetto mansion-
No other place I would live

In my ghetto mansion
You will always be comfortable
My ghetto mansion-
I will make you special company

Steak and eggs may be
The order of a day
My door is open everyday
You are welcome—always

Myles W. Wallace

My Life, My Love, I Give You My Everything

I live my life just for you
You make my world turn
My sun to view

You are sweetness
The morning rising
You are the sunset
On my horizon

You make the stars
Twinkle in the night
Without you
I would not have daylight

The moon is always full
With you
Radiating with
Shimmering beauty

My world would not exist
Without you
You keep my life
So refreshingly new

My Love Is More Real Than Imagined

In your world of fantasy
The earth of make-believe
You tell me my love doesn't exist
I stand here before you
To say, right now, honey
Your tenderness I miss

I don't think of anyone
Except, you-love
My mind is cloud nine
You are the love of my life
That is the top line

Your phone I constantly ring
Flowers I will always bring

My love is more real than imagined
It is more than a genie
My love is more real than imagined
Darling, it is you I am feeling

My heart is in wonderland
With abundant euphoria
When I speak your name, sugar
I am on top of utopia

A wander through the park,
With you, makes it my isle of pleasure
We don't have to stop
To taste the cotton candy
Baby, you are my sweet treasure

I envision us on a journey
Cruising through the milky way
We are locked in a elated embrace
Totally absorbed with each other
Savoring distant space

Myles W. Wallace

You are my girl
Beyond—this world

My love is more real than imagined
Truly conceived
Baby, my love is more real than imagined
Darling, you are all that I need

My Love, Doll Baby

Fine as wine
Sweet peppermint snap
Silk legged lady
Good as a government check

She flows in splendor
Regal queen
Perfectly majestic
I'm her king

I'm on top when near her
My love, doll baby
I get high when I hear her
My love, doll baby

It started with a kiss
Blossomed in the light
This kaleido love
Renewed my life

She's got bouncing wavy hair
Natural in style
Her hip hugging jeans
Know their way around

Jubilation is our atmosphere
Her star is my light
Smiling sunshine
She does everything just right

She's a lady with
High self-esteem
Who finds time to boogie
And always is for real

I turn on when I give her
My love, doll baby
I am true to win her
My love, doll baby

Myles W. Wallace

My Ten Demerits Of Love

Like the ten commandments of love
I have ten demerits of love
Let me explain
I will start with number one

Running off at the mouth
Keeps one in trouble
Which could eventually turn into
A busted bubble

The second demerit is; playing around
Especially if the news
Echoes around town

The third demerit is;
Being tight with money
Which directly leads to
Big and deep trouble

Number four is;
Messing up food
That is a perfect reason
To get cut loose

The fifth one is;
Holding back when we make love
Our relationship would surely result in
A total dud

There are ten demerits of love
These are my first five
If you are still with me
I will run the second half by

Numeral six;
Putting my business in the street
That will escalate into
Irreversible defeat

Demerit number seven;
Being a phony friend
With me that is definitely
The bitter end

Number eight;
Standing me up
Do it once
Hey!, I've had enough

And number nine;
Riding your black stallion
Being pompous and prissy
To me that is incomprehensible

Finally, number ten:
Be true to yourself
I'm human, I make mistakes
Hopefully, not one
That will mean heartache

My ten demerits of love
Pertain to life
If you use them wisely
They are sound advice

Myles W. Wallace

My Thoughts Of You Turned To Love

When we first met
I wanted to be more than friends
Now that it has happened
Our love will have no end

With our first kiss
There was a special feeling
You were so sweet
My mind reacted immediately

My thoughts of you turned to love
Sure as in day there is light
My thoughts of you turned to love
I wanted to kiss you all night

My life I have searched for you
Your love I have always sought
My heart was the first to know
Our paths would somehow cross

Every second that ticks by
Of you I dream
My emotions fill the sky
You will be my love eternally

My thoughts of you turned to love
It's glow is star bright
My thoughts of you turned to love
Our love is just right

Night

When we were together
My life was filled with sunshine
You left without reason
Never again to be mine

Loving moments together
Made my life glow
No more moonlit walks
I need only one ticket
For the picture show

Night—The dark side of time
Night—Back of the line

Walls close in
The vacuum in which I exist
I am trapped
I feel like a satellite adrift
Rejected from the mothership

I search for your love
To guide my way
So that I may be safe
Oblique images
Divert—block—sway

Night—On me it fell
Night—Distance tells

No One Will Love You (The Why I Do)

Love will come
Love may go
You may chose
You can know

I will put you on a pedestal
Our love will grow
No one will bring us down
We will ascend to a higher goal

No obstacle will block our path
I will clear the road
Any other distraction
Will be on permanent hold

No one will ever love you (The way I do)
My feelings are real
No one will ever love you (The way I do)
My words are sincere

Business works to keep us apart
Prevents our holding one another
There is so much love in our hearts
We understand each other

If competition dares to take me on
It's best they stand fast
Absolutely, there will be no changes
Denigrating our romance

We are going to be together
Through lifes' trials and tribulations
My commitment is forever
To keep you without reservation

No one will ever love you (The way I do)
My adoration will never falter
No one will ever love you (The way I do)
My revelation is above the altar

Nobody To trust, No One To Love

I left home
At an early age
No one was there to guide me

Now, as an adult
It is more—the same
I need someone beside me

Nobody to trust, nobody to love
The story of my life
Nobody to trust, nobody to love
I need advice

I am a wanderer
Just who am I?
I have no destiny
Life's messages I don't identify

The tunnel's light
Awaits my touch
I reach out—but
I can't hold long enough

Myles W. Wallace

Nothing But A Star

The lady I marry
Make her a star
My lifetime I have waited
To be a part

I want to wake in the morning
Look at her lovely smile
I like going to bed and
Doing it in style

Nothing but a star
That is all I want
Nothing but a star
One who is choice

I know she will be sweet
And genuinely nice
She will love me
She will give me advice

She will not flirt
With her I will never be alone
She will be my company
When she not at home

Nothing but a star
That is how I feel
Nothing but a star
Someone real

Now It's Time To Cry

I was busy
I did not know you were gone
I was so preoccupied
I could not believe
To another you belonged

You are most important to me
Along with school and work
Our love lost balance
Not by fate or quirk

Now it's time to cry
No need to ask myself why
It's time to cry
Three days after you said goodbye

Reconciliation might work
I just don't have time
I have meetings to attend
With other situations beside

It's time cry
To myself I cannot lie
Now it's time to cry
Love has passed me by

Obsessed

I want you honey
I want you darling
In a sweet sensuous way
I want you baby!
My love is here to stay

I want to hold you close
Squeeze you tight
Touch you nice

I want to make love with you
Both day and night

Baby, I'm obsessed with you
I want no other
Sweetheart, I'm obsessed with you
Your love I covet

You are on my mind
Twenty-four hours—everyday
I daydream and sleepwalk you
You love will never go away

I rise with you each morning
The sun won't melt my love away
I see your pretty face on billboards
When I ride the expressways

Every night I go to sleep
With you on my mind
I never forget you
Not for one second of time

Sugar I am obsessed with you
Surely your love comes from above
Oh baby! I am obsessed with you
It is my—blood

Sweetheart I am obsessed with you
I have lost all control
Honey I am obsessed with you
Your love is my soul

Oh! Beautiful Love

Breasts to chest
Eye to eye contact
Hands—caressing
Orgasms back to back

Sweat pouring bodies
Hair tousled about
Walls resonate screaming
Compassion all around

The bare truth self-evident
While we are intimate
Life becomes relevant

Oh! Beautiful love
Oh! Oh! Oh!
Ah! Beautiful love
More and more and more

Legs wrapped waist high
Rapid fire injection
Accelerated pulsing
There is no hesitation

We are one
Never separate
Hearts beat time
The world we escape

Lips touch
Tongues embraced
A single mind
Comprises our state

Oh! Beautiful love
For souls existence
Oh! Beautiful love
Ever—more uplifting

Myles W. Wallace

Oil

Black gold, Texas tea
Nature's gift to woman and man
It can be found under water
Or beneath land

Oil provides humankind
With many useful products
From asphalt to vinyl
When it is gone
It will be complete and final

Imports and exports produce
Enormous profits
For human dependency
We have no option

Perhaps it is possible
That our destinies are
One in the same
We have glory now
Then go out in a flame

Once A Knight, That's Enough For Me

Once a king, always a king
Once a knight
That's enough for me

My woman likes to do it for
Hours at a time
I can't keep it up
That's the bottom line

She is always ready
Just how I like her to be
But once I let go
That's it!—You see

Once a king, always a king
Once a knight
That's enough for me

She has got good stuff
Don't get me wrong
I just can't hang
Not for long

When I jump in
Instantly I cut loose
The snapper she's got
She knows how to use

Once a king, always a king
Once a knight
Hey, that's enough for me!

One Fell Swoop Of Your Love

Out of the clear blue sky
You came like a hawk in pursuit
Talons stretched out
To run was of no use

Though I never stumbled
Nor did I sway
I seemed, someway, somehow
To be your only prey

One fell swoop of your love
I knew I would be captured
One fell swoop of your love
I was enraptured

The summer winds that day
Caused your sweet smell
To permeate the air

Your graceful beauty
Descended on me
My attraction was
More powerful than gravity

Your arms were like wings
That held me firm
Your body soft as feathers
Was filled with warmth
My heart began to sing

One fell swoop of your love and
The seed of love had been planted
One fell swoop of your love
Made my love grow faster

P.S. I Love You

As I write this letter
I think about the end
Things could have been better
But this game I just couldn't win

I had the opportunity for love
It looks like I failed
I don't think I meant much to you
It was like swinging the hammer
And missing the nail

Was it that I care too much
You know this to be true
I thought we had everything;
Love, security, trust
But you say you didn't love me
Those were harsh words coming from you

They say, if you don't succeed
To try again
I have loved and lost
You are too far gone
It looks like the end

I feel like I have been doublecrossed
But, I realize I still care
For better or worse
P.S. I love you
I will always want you here

Myles W. Wallace

Pain

Not the prick of a pin
The cut with a knife
Yes, the worst hurt of all
The derailment of my life

Material things you can have
Take the money—run
Just remember this
My heart contains your love

I feel pain, worse than any ache
Pain, since you have gone away
Pain, dilutes my pride
Pain, the way I feel inside

There is throbbing in my head
A shock to my chest
I'm weak in the knees
I cannot get any rest

With you, I was on top
I can't pull myself together
Now that you are gone
The bottom has dropped out

I feel pain, a forest without rain
Pain, no light in the day
Pain, a soundless wave
Pain, a face without a name

Papa Bear (Football Strike)

In his tower he sat
Gazing—nowhere particular
A smile creased his face
When he began reminiscing

Red Grange
Galloped through his mind
Sid Luckman
Brilliantly passed
Bronco Nugurski
Blocked and tackled
Willie Galimore—Ran

Suddenly a scowl crossed Papa Bear's face
Blurting—"Football Strike!"
"These people loved the game
It was their life"

"Some performed with leather helmets
Others had meager contracts
They would show up early
Even for practice"

"Today, it's million dollar salaries
Exclusive-bonus contracts
Free Agency—Lawyers
Owners stand—fight!"

The old man eased back in his chair
Knew he was in the driver's seat
It still riled him
Todays' players-elite

Johnnie Morris
Dazzled his brain
Gayle Sayers
Exhibited fame
Dick Butkus
Banged and mauled
Mike Ditka—Blazed

Papa Bear jumped straight up
This strike really had his goat
He began shaking his fists
Speaking loudly as he paced the floor

"I've been with this game
All of my years
A football strike
For what purpose"

"Ok—Players get bumped and bruised
But, they are well paid
The average career is just 48 months
They also get a pension"

"No matter what they think
I don't see their rationale
If I were 20 years younger
Heck—I'd play myself!"

With those soothing thoughts
George Halas opened the window
Rain splashed his face
Acknowledging unseasonable conditions

In his tower he sat
Gazing—nowhere particular
A smile creased his brow
Papa Bear began—reminiscing

Paper Love

It's the kind of love
That makes me jump through hoops
The type of love
That throws me a loop

It's a feeling
That keeps me high
With meaning
That lets my mind fly

I love you
I am afraid
To say it in your face

I adore you
I write letters and poems
I communicate better, this way

Don't be afraid
It's only paper love
You can crumple me
Throw me away

I'm only paper love
It's only words
I want to say

Your touch of love
Makes me hear bells
It's a brand of love
That keeps my chest swelled

A sensation
That causes me to lose control
An emotion
Deep in my soul

I care for you
A conversation I can't hold on the phone
My words get caught in my throat
I start to tremble
Can't go on

It's just paper love
Romantic fairy tales
If only they would come true
Together we would have it made
Into the horizon we would sail

Perfect

You don't live in a penthouse
Or drive a fancy car
You are understanding, sweet
You're perfect
Perfect to me

You don't make a million a year
Or own a boutique
You have a caring heart, a loving smile
You're perfect
Perfect to me

You don't need shoulder length hair
Or a model's waist
You are kind, sensitive
You're perfect
Perfect to me

You don't need an hour glass figure
Or a P.H.D.
You are beautiful, pretty
You are perfect
Perfect for me

You are a wonderful person to know
A young lady on the move
Star, on the go

You make my life complete
You're my lady elite
Darling, you are perfect for me

Myles W. Wallace

Perfect To Love

Beaded hair
Painted toes
Pretty lips
Sparkling eyes
You are my dream come true
Your style I idolize

Your touch is that of
A fluent artist
Sweet kisses
Truly earnest

When you smile
Its a luminous addition
If I talk
Intently you listen

You are perfect to love
Cultured lady
Perfect to love
Chocolate favor

Dinner you prepare
Gourmet sauteed
Your domicile is immaculate
With candles ingeniously placed

Love you perform
In a carefree manner
Your charm is my hearts'
My waving banner

Perfect to love
Princess of sharing
Perfect to love
You are alluringly understanding

Playing Hard To Get

When I call
You are always gone
You tell me to come by
When you are not alone

We make a date and
You never show
I want to go and party
You say take it slow

You are playing hard to get
Like a pass to a receiver
Playing hard to get
You smart deceiver

You are more illusive
Than Harry Houdini
You disappear for weeks
I only see you if I am dreaming

You make an appearance
To keep me in check
Then, away you go
Leaving me a nervous wreck

You are playing hard to get
You little heart stealer
You are playing hard to get
You clever wheeler dealer

Myles W. Wallace

Poems Of My Life

Nature had the first
Followed by man
Then came radio, next television
Succeeded by satellite transmissions
That cover all lands

Orchestras display musical form
Choirs provide substance
Lyrics give a clue
Like bees make honey

Poems of my life
They are all around
Poems of my life
Beautiful sounds

A baying retriever
A purring cat
Chirping crickets
Even decamping bats

Rushing water
Racing winds
The rising sun
Returning friends

A rapid vehicle
And flashing trains
A booming jetliner
Or bulging sails

Poems are my life
They keep me informed
Poems of my life
Pleasure they have shown

Portrait Of A Lonely Man

See the picture
Surrounded by a frame
The photograph shows a man
With his head hanging

In this pix
There is a flower
The sole possession
For the man of the hour

This is a picture of an secluded lad
The portrait of a lonely man
The cameo of a youth so sad
A portrait of a lonely man

Up against the world
One may think
Just him
The lower he sinks

The rose
That he clutches tightly
Is his link to happiness
Through the Almighty

The etching of an isolated stand
Portrait of a lonely man
A sketch of a repulsed plan
The portrait of a lonely man

Myles W. Wallace

Pretty Baby

Pretty baby
Will you be mine
For me to shine

Pretty baby
You make me glow
For your show

Pretty baby
Your kind heart
I want to be a part
I feel your love afar
I will be your shining star

Pretty baby

Pretty baby
Don't ever go away
My heart would be an empty space

Pretty baby

Pretty baby
I will hold you sweet
Pretty baby
You mean the world to me

Pretty baby
You will always be top
My caring will never stop

Pretty baby
My mind is your number one slot
My love won't ever stop

Pretty baby

Price Tag

Everything has a cost
Don't you ever mistake meekness
Because I treat you well
As a substitute for weakness

I buy you nice things
I give you money too
But, you take my love for granted
Apathy is your view

All I want is to
Just be your friend
Which I have a hard time doing
Because, your complaining never ends

There is a price tag on everything
So what!, If I have to be alone
There is a price tag on all things
If you don't stop griping
I will be long gone

You talk about what I eat
Yet, your refrigerator is bare
You don't like the way I dress
Or even comb my hair

You say I don't exercise enough
I should learn how to jog
But your bicycle is broken
Aerobics you won't try

Your criticism is never constructive
It is meant to bring down
You like to see me suffer
Because, someone stole your heart

There is a price tag on everything
Just wait, you'll see
There is a price tag on all things
When you end up losing me

Myles W. Wallace

Private Citizen

My Your On Business is my motto
Serenity is my world
Idle chatter—gossip
Disturbs my nerves

I do like parties
A few I participate
Just with soft music
I have a mild drink

I am Private Citizen U.S.A.
Private Citizen, that I will say

Bustling crowds
I constantly avoid
I shun attention
I cannot stand the noise

It bothers me
When the telephone rings
If I do not answer the door
Please don't make a scene

I am Private Citizen—whisper
Private Citizen, Hush. Now listen

Put The Pressure On The Perpetrators

They break and enter
Then they want to jack you up
They take everything you own
When you are down on your luck

If you call the authorities
Nowhere they can be found
Then the thugs threaten you
Saying: "You better leave town"

Put the pressure on the perpetrators
You can't depend on the law
Put the pressure on the perpetrators
Everything you hear is talk

Let me tell you what I would do
If I were in those shoes
First, I would launch a couple of rounds
And tell the oafs—vamoose

If they did not take heed
Next, I would let them have my boot
And if that had no effect
Finally, I would have to cut loose

Put the pressure on the perpetrators
Make it the bottom line
Put the pressure on the perpetrators
Because they do the crimes

It is so bad day and night
You cannot walk down the street
Or go to the local store
Lurking in the shadows
They all carry a big piece

Their patterns are random
Although they always seem to be around
You can never catch them
They are never found

Put the pressure on the perpetrators
They really have a lot of nerve
Put the pressure on the perpetrators
A stiff sentence is what they deserve

What about the ones
Who call themselves "professionals"
Greed is their crime
Think about it for a second
They still mess up human lives

Let's give these neophytes
A taste of their own medicine
Pitch them all in jail
That is one way of reducing
The expanding crime wave

Put the pressure on the perpetrators
Change the locks and throw away the keys
Put the pressure on the perpetrators
Life should be crime free

Rambling Of A Madman

Decisions, Indecision, Fidelity,
Conclusions, Delusions, Confusion,
Gasoline, Prices, Inflation,
Confidence, Coercion, Collusion
Crime, Incest, Pornography,
War, Greed, Photography,
Aches, Pains, Medicine,
Calculators, Sliderules, Pushbuttons,
Rockets, Missiles, Bombs,
Recession, Depression, Jobs,
Traffic, Congestion, Anger,
Home, Relax, Tension,
Telephone, Bells, Banging,
Motors, Alarms, Clanging,
Lightning, Thunder, Raining,
Walking, Running, Playing,
Bible, Libel, Tribal,
Skates, Wheels, Circles,
Jumping, Hitting, Stalking,
Clocks, Punch, Whistle,
Rate, Produce, Bogey,
Pencil, Pen, Xerox,
Manuals, Books, Posters,
People, Persons, Collectors,
Mail, Shop, Sending,
Love, Hate, Jealousy,
Conquests, Contrive, Console,
Help, Hurt, Handclap,
Kiss, Cuddle, Fondle,
Favor, Fake, Forget,
Television, Radio, Satellite,
Nomination, Election, Vote,
School, Work, Pray,
Dog, Cat, Joke

Myles W. Wallace

Reserve

He comes out the stands
From behind the glass
To accommodate her
When she wants to prance

He will come off the bench
Without as much as a flinch
To take her out
For a pinch

He is a reserve
He plays all positions
For the number one spot
He constantly wishes

He is a utility man
A jack-of-all-trades
With the drop of a pin
He will go to her aid

He is a third stringer
A fill-in
A perennial last place finisher
He never wins

He is a reserve
A back door man
An outside cad
He is just a fad

Resistance

Resistance is—
Saying no
Instead of speaking yes

Resistance is—
Not trying
When you could do your best

Resistance is—
Walking
When you should run

Resistance is—
Sulking
When you could have fun

Resistance is—
Laying back
Not being real
Trying to play cool
Living in a world of make-believe

Resistance is—
Laughing
When you should be crying
It is holding on
When you should say goodbye

Myles W. Wallace

Restrictions

The runway is so long
As buildings are tall
The freeway is so wide
Contained with walls

The sun shines only
Part of the day
Night is near
No time to play

Restrictions—they are life
Restrictions—keep things tight

Money does not go far
Materialism has limits
People are abundant
Work isn't

You can ascend
Just to go out
The Peter Principle applies
A no-win bout

Restrictions—to the top
Restrictions—then you stop

Rich Man's Laugh

He laughs uproariously loud
And it's all with a tainted smile

His diamond covered hands
Try to cover his mouth

As his overstuffed belly
Jiggles from north to south

His robe is draped
Down to his knees

And his lap dog
Knows not what is defeat

His silver covered feet are kicked
High in the air

As he looks out of his window
Cause in this world
He doesn't have a care

His overlong cigar is spewing smoke
All over the place

He has a clear view of everything
And there are no tears in his face

He hardly knows where he is
In his gold covered room
And he could care less

Life is not his problem
Wanna bet?

Myles W. Wallace

Run, Jesse, Run

Pistol firing, Pow!

They're off and running
Look: There's a populist in this prestigious race
Who could it be—non other than
Mister Jesse L. Jackson
A man content of character, and candidate for
The highest office of this land
The 1984 President of the United States

Out of a field of thousands
Forty men have won this contest
But, Jesse Jackson is the only man
Who has his heart invested

With his firm handshake, assuring smile
This loving—family man
Has his own dedicated style

In the Democratic Primary he entered last
But, he will move swiftly—to the front
Passing all the non-contenders
With a strong platform-performance

Agitators yell; He's unqualified
Arguments the constitution rejects
Thirty-five years of age
And a U.S. citizen, the document states

Other critics say he doesn't have
A snowballs chance for winning
And he his little campaign money
Heroes they want to put down
Jesse Jackson is a leader,
He will be the front runner

Jesse Jackson eloquently speaks the truth
This charismatic country preacher
Expresses peoples views

Jesse Lewis Jackson says he will choose
A lady, Vice Presidential running mate
It has never been before
Reverend Jesse Jackson does not discriminate

Some may consider him
The dark horse of this race
That is a choice
For all unbiased voters to make

Run, Jesse, Run
Run for the aged, the weak, the young
Run, Jesse, Run
Run for the sick, handicapped, poor
Run, Jesse, Run
Run for our Mothers, Fathers, Sisters, Brothers
Run, Jesse, Run
Run for the people of the world
To become allied with each other

Some say segregation has passed
You can live where you want
After Six P.M.
Just be careful where you walk

You can go to any school you choose
That is, if you can afford
Which is especially difficult
If you don't have room and board

Heat or eat is
A very desperate situation
That is the choice
When you're a victim of deprivation

Medias persistently tell us
The economy is—up
The recession is bottoming out
And unemployment is going down
Most young people, this nation's future
Have never had a job
Experience is not theirs' to be found

Jails are despairingly full of black men
Americans are fighting, losing their lives overseas
Rampant teenage pregnancies-
It is a tumultuous plea

Run, Jesse, Run
Run for jobs, justice, peace
Run, Jesse, Run
Run for the disadvantaged, poverty torn, our beliefs
Run, Jesse, Run
Run for children, housing, education
Run, Jesse, Run
Run, for humanity, equality, faith

A multitude of our African Ancestors
Were thrown overboard overcrowded ships
Those that did survive, met a mean whip
On this soil, long we toiled for unpaid dues
Now we must take advantage of opportunity anew

Hooded villains, poll taxes, grandfather clauses
Did not turn us from the vote
Registration, legislation—mandates
Proof—positive results

Reconstruction meant temporary power
Which was more than four-score ago
We don't want nobody to give us nothing
Just open the door

One man, one vote
I think the opposition understands
If now is not the time to run—then when?

Run, Jesse, Run
Run for every man, every woman, every child
Run, Jesse, Run
Every second, minute, every hour
Run, Jesse, Run
Run for King, Medgar, Malcolm X
Run, Jesse, Run
Run for SCLC, Push, Core and SNCC

There won't be much of a world left to live in
If nuclear proliferation has its say
Preservation of this earth would succeed
When Jesse Jackson intervenes and
Let the survivalists have their way

Run, Jesse, Run
Glide—pass the Republican designate
Run, Jesse, Run
It's the soul of humankind—you represent

Run, Jesse, Run
History you'll defeat
Win, Jesse, Win!
Win, Jesse, Win!
I am somebody
At last—we will be free!

Myles W. Wallace

Sad Eyes

Sad eyes all around
Sad eye—Uptown

Sad eyes asking questions
Sad eyes reveal uncertainty

For moments of happiness
They would surely wink
With hours of gloom
They don't even blink

They have not given up
Opportunity will strike
They will latch on
To never turn back

Sad eyes full of hope
Sad eyes show soul

Sad eyes see above
Sad eyes are love

Save Those Goodbyes For My Return

At the airport—we kiss and hug
You say you don't want to see me go
If somehow I didn't come back
You couldn't run the show

We become one
As arms circle waists
The crowd is staring
Our love is with respect

The kind of love I'm receiving
You never loved me this way before
Even when we were making love
Behind closed and bolted doors

I'm not suspicious
Jealous, I never was
But, the way you are treating me now
Save those goodbyes for my return

You hold me like a good sleeping pillow
Your body is fire
You squeeze my hand, tightly
Say, I'm your only desire

I slowly board the plane
I see you smiling through the window
Tears are streaming down your face
You are waving, furiously

I will only be gone a week
You said it will feel like years
Just don't go any place
Save those goodbyes for my return

Myles W. Wallace

Say What You Feel

If your boss acts like a jerk
Call him that
You can't get along with your neighbor?
Don't tap him on the back

If someone doesn't treat you fair
Don't mumble under your breath
If you deserved an "A" on the exam
Speak out—don't guess

Say what you feel
Don't bite your tongue
Say what mean
Don't hold a grudge

If your morning is bad
Don't say "good!"
If you are having a problem
Acknowledge it—be sure

If you don't feel like being bothered
Express your mind
Are you tired of your company?
Tell them: "Goodbye!"

Say what you feel
Don't hold back
Say what you mean
Stop being matter-of-fact

Scared The Yell Out Of Me

I thought my baby left
I dreamed she was gone
My mind has not been right
Since my heart left home

She has been coming home
After work—late
My mind babbled—
"Baby is on a date"

It scared the yell out of me
My soul was sick
It scared the pure de yell out of me
Worse than any horror flick

Am I guilty of being jealous
Or is this a premonition
For the pain I might experience

I will not get excited
I will use common sense
The togetherness we have
Tells me there is no need for suspense

It still scared the yell out of me
I thought I had an attack
Yeah, it scared the living yell out of me
I am happy my lady is back

"Scorpio"

He was born at the age of ten
Unofficially, he's almost two
That's not what his teachers exclaimed
When they asked him to leave nursery school

You see, Scorpio is an adult
Captured in a child's body
He just can't convince anyone
That he knows anything about it

Scorpio is smart and doesn't like to play
He knows he's in command
He won't let you get next to him
To seize the upper hand

Now, mother knows him best
Although, he thinks he has her fooled
Mom's the boss
She is the one who made all the rules

Scorpio is a leader
He only lacks experience
He makes up for that by
Being charming—fearless

It won't take long for
Scorpio to become a man
In his mind he already is
Just ask the young ladies—when he's near

Mom is keeping a watchful eye
She doesn't want him to learn too fast
She tells him: "Son, one day at a time
That is the only way it will fit into my plans"

Scorpio, manchild or boywonder?
Precocious one might say
No matter how grown he acts
He will always be mommy's baby

Scream, Scream, Scream

The speaker is doing his thing
Reality is just a shattered dream
Scream, Scream, Scream

Locally the situation is the same
I did my year for the man
Scream, scream, scream

Employment is just a word
Man, give me my thunderbird
Scream, scream, scream

School are hollowed halls
Save the children—that's all
Scream, scream, scream

Revolution is that the solution
Is there any air pollution

Ha, Ha, Ha, Ha, Ha, Ha, Ha . . . .

♥ *Secret* ♥

What is this secret you carry around
That you don't want anyone to know
What is this secret you keep
That you won't let yourself go

Your conversations are always brief,
Straight to the point
You won't let them flow

Your visits are quick and
You are always in a hurry to
Rush out the door

What is your secret
Please tell me
I won't tell anyone else

I want to know your secret
So that I can put
My sanity to rest

Did you hit the lotto?
Your ship came in?
Are you going away
To never come back again?

Does it involve business?
Is it a personal condition?
Or is it a new investment?
Possibly a romantic situation?

I have got to know your secret!
I have to know it right now!
Not knowing your secret
Keeps my mind in a cloud!

♥

Shocked

Thunder can't shake me
Lightning won't wake me
From love that escapes me
Happiness was a break for me

We were inseparable
Almost twins
A third party entered the picture
Romance began to skid

I'm shocked
Like a stranger's knock
A pistol shot

Shocked,
The smash of a rock
Glass dropped

An earthquake won't rouse me
An institution can't house me
From pain that clouds me
Joy no longer bounds me

We were one
Our lives filled with fun
Now, I am at the bottom
No longer your charm

I'm shocked
A car that can't stop
An empty birthday box

Shocked,
Like a karate chop
A broken lock

Shocked,
A shirt with a spot
A sentence without a dot

I'm shocked
My love is out
It makes me shout!

Show You're Right

Do a good deed
Someone needs help
Most of all
Respect yourself

Put on the spotlight
To highlight yourself
Turn up the stage lamps
Illuminate your values

Show you're right
Be true to yourself
Show you're right
You are the best

To the top of the world
You will rise
Then form your view
Of the other side

Don't let anyone
Bring you down
Stick out your chest
Be real proud

Show you're right
Use your advice
Show you're right
Take control of your life

Skeletons In Your Closet

Did you do something wrong
And your conscience is bothering you
Now you have got something to hide
Which is bad news

Maybe you said something you should not
Or you kept something you should not have
Perhaps you neglected a good deed
And wouldn't lend a helping hand

You have skeletons in your closet
Income Tax
You have skeletons in your closet
Distorted facts

Did you tell a lie
Because you were in a hurry
Did you not stand up
When someone needed your to courage

Did you run from a scene
Where you were a witness
Now locked in your room
Who are you kidding

You have got skeletons in your closet
And nowhere to go
With skeletons in your closet
The public knows

Myles W. Wallace

Slowdown

You live every second
As if it were your last
You move every minute
Going nowhere fast

The right goals you have to succeed
Motivation you definitely possess
Achievement is your admirable trait
Awareness is your best

Slowdown, baby
Let life come to you
Slowdown, sugar
Persistence will see you through

Hold your horses
Just don't hesitate
Keep your momentum going
Take life day by day

The honor roll you will rule
Graduation is near
Awards you will reap
Now is the time to cheer

Slowdown, honey
Enjoy every hour
Slowdown, baby
Your success is now

Something Is Wrong With That Picture

I see hugging and kissing
Lots of touching—playing
A bunch of laughing, prancing
Even more swinging and swaying

I see hands around waists
Face in face
Fingers running through hair
Man and woman embraced

There's something wrong with that picture
Something's not quite right
Maybe there is not enough light

There's something wrong with that picture
I just can't figure it out
The scene leaves me in doubt

I see hand holding
Long walks in the park
I hear midnight conversations
Whispering after dark

I see boat rides
Parties on the beach
Lots of activity
Out of my reach

There's something wrong with that picture
Are they looking at me
Smiling, calm as can be

There's something wrong with my picture
Oh! Now I get it
The something wrong with my picture is
I'm not in it!

Myles W. Wallace

Somewhere Down The Line (You Will Love Me)

Why don't you come by my house
I mean my apartment
I said my room
I am staying with friends
Because I'm down and out

A Mercedes you drive
I have a push-mobile
If your does not start
I will be there to
Transport you uphill

Although I am on my last leg
And you are at the top
I need you here now
To share your warmth

You are beautiful, famous and rich
I am just a man
I love you
One day you will understand

Because, somewhere down the line
You will see my love as true
Some where down the line
My love is special, just for you

A college education you have
I am just a high-school grad
I have seen your class ring
Something I have never had

You work in a glass tower
I am a clerk in a five and dime store
You dine out every night
Coupons litter my kitchen floor

Somewhere down the line
(You will love me)
I will stay in your sight
Somewhere down the line
(You will love me)
Because, you are my life

Myles W. Wallace

Spellbound

I'm hypnotized
You performed sorcery
Totally mesmerized
By your wonderful wizardry

With a crystal ball
You emerged as a fortune teller
A bright future you foretold
Like a genie appears brilliant

I'm spellbound
You are my prophet
I'm spellbound
Truly, you are a messiah

The stars revealed
An angel you follow
With your eminent wisdom
You're also an inimitable scholar

You engaged my mind
Like a metronome clock
You predicted joy
Happiness is your watch

I'm spellbound
You possess a magician's wand
I'm spellbound
You are my golden charm

Starring You

The curtains open
Starring you
The flood lights shine
Starring you

You are a thespian and
You appear on my matinee
You belong on every set
I desire you for every play

The theater is yours
The platform concerns you too
The scene is one of romance
As we begin act ii

This is our greatest performance
Starring you
Better than Shakespeare
Starring you

The role will always be yours
You were cast as new
The script contains lines
Developed only for you

The skit is simple
Accompanied by a symphony
Your walk on presentation
Will be proceeded by a timpani

The curtains part
Starring you
The floodlights shine
Starring you

Myles W. Wallace

Stormtrooper Love

I want to zero in on you
Just like they drop a bomb
Like machine gun Kelly
I'm aiming for your heart

I'm talking about that stormtrooper love

There's no giving up for me
Like a kimakazee
I'll love you forever and better
Because I'm a madman about you see

I'm talking about that stormtrooper love

I'll be as fast as a triggerman
Love is where I'm coming from
I'll be good as a henchman
Going straight for your mind like gangbusters

I'm talking about that stormtrooper love

Just like racket squad
I'll be gung ho
I'm going to give you everything I got
Like a hatchet man I'll go with the throw

Oh yeah, that stormtrooper love

Straight Line

There is a saying that goes
The shortest distance between two points
Is a straight line
That expression fits perfectly
For a meeting of our minds

I do not like to beat around the world
So I will get right to my point
I want to make love with you
You look so good
I know you are choice

I know you want a say in this matter
Yes, you have every right
Just make it in a few seconds
I want to spend the remaining time
With you tonight

Baby, I am coming to you in a straight line
Just like an archers' arrow
In a straight line
Swift and narrow

I realize the way I am approaching
You may want to run and hide
I am determined to get you
—A targets' bulls-eye

Do not worry, I am not going hurt you
I have an experts' touch
And girl, when I shoot my best shot
On me you will definitely have a crush

I do not want to possess you
Like some illustrious won prize
But when you came into view
You really caught my mind

In a straight line
That is how my love will fly
In a straight line
I am aiming for your heart
That is why I know you will be mine

Stretch Marks

My lady has fine thin lines
That circle her tummy and hips

Not too long ago
Into the world she brought a new baby
With a bit of my assistance

I am very proud of our child
I look forward to being with baby everyday
That is the reason I don't complain about anything
That pertains to my love's body way

Stretch marks—They look so beautiful to me
Stretch marks—Display motherhood splendidly

Together we exercise, since we both gained a few pounds
While waiting for the stork to arrive
Now I'm not one who likes to jump up and down
But, it pleases my lady, so I will stay by her side

Stretch marks—Keep us together
Stretch marks—Make us better

Whether my lady wears a suit, dress or bikini
She styles them breathtakingly
My mind has no doubt, that she is the one for me

Stretch marks—Have a family touch
Stretch marks—To me they mean so much

Stud

He gives it to them
A few inches at a time
Until he blows their minds
Just before this occurs
They shout his name
Which is stud

They love to come with him
It is always with a sudden thud
He is a the complete Casanova
He never shrugs
Because he is stud

No matter what entrance
He strolls into a room
Eyes left and right
Check out his pud
He is so self-assured
Another reason
They call him stud

When he struts his stuff
Up and down the street
Or even jumps in his ride
There is always
An obvious bud
Now you see why
They call him stud

Myles W. Wallace

Stunned

I feel like a runner who won the race
And his prize was—second place

I feel like a ship who found its way
Then vanishes suddenly without a trace

Stunned like an electric shock
Stunned like a pistol pops

Stunned—a child without play
A missing yesterday

Stunned like a wasp's sting
Stunned—an interrupted dream
Stunned—cornbread with no greens
Hog mog without black eye peas

Love came, then you left
Like winning fourth place in lotto
It was not the best

I tried to convince you
Love deserved another chance
You turned away, said
I wasn't a first place man

I'm stunned like a empty dinner pot
Stunned like a dentist's shot

Stunned like rice with no starch
Stunned—soldiers that can't march

Stunned—summer and no road construction
A rabbit without reproduction

I'm stunned

Take It Off Baby, Take It All Off

When you came by my pad
You were dressed from head to toe
I mean from your ankle bracelet
To your large wig-a-la afro

I wanted you to be comfortable
So that we could really get down
I started with your necklace
And your frown turned into a smile

You turned toward me
Whispered hotly in ear
Take it off baby, take it all off
Take it off baby, take it all off

When you said that
I began to work faster and faster
I grabbed your pantyhose
And tore out the elastic

Your shoes were what
I went after next
And by this time
I was just about a nervous wreck

You grabbed me by my neck
Which seemed like for life
I couldn't help but hang on
And take your advice

Take it off baby, take it all off
Take it off baby, take it all off

To your girdle
I came ever so near
You put a mild struggle
But your message was moist and clear

With my hand in your waistband
You kissed me gently
I said have no fear
Then your motion became erratic
And with your tongue in my ear

You said: Take it off baby, take it all off
Oh baby, take it off, take it all off

I had you there
Like in the world, the day you came
There were no more clothes left
I made your claim

You were all mine
In your mind there was no doubt
When we made love
You said: Please don't ever stop

I looked it you and grinned
Then I said: I took it off baby
I took it all off
Oh yeah, I took it off baby
I took it all off
From bottom to top

Ten Minute Kiss

I ask you for a kiss
You have such sweet pretty lips
I know we will enjoy
This I am convinced

It is the first time we kiss
Something I always wanted to do
While sitting on my sofa
You say you want me to

Our lips touch
Soul on soul
I am in another world
My heart has taken control

I see visions
Gold and pearls
I do everything within my power
To keep holding on

I see rainbow colors
I feel above the clouds
We guide in unison
My head feels like it is
Spinning round and round

I feel your back arch
Your eyes appear—glazed
I don't know up from down
My mind is hazed

We are embraced
Our hearts beat as one
Probing and pulsing
Are our tongues

Myles W. Wallace

I peek, just for a moment
You are in ecstasy
We have become one
Our bonding is replete

I have roaming hands
You have rushing fingers
We can't let go
This is real life-dreaming

It seems like a lifetime
That we became one
Just a ten minute kiss
Love won

Thank God

The alarm clock wakes you
You say: "Good job"
This is the best time to
Thank God

You praise the pilot saying
"The plane did not go down"
You should look up and say
Thank God

You've got money, materialism
Your family is top-notch
You've never been seriously ill
Thank God

Perseverance brings you through
Crisis you don't dodge
You have His assurance
Thank God

He is your friend
He exceeds all odds
This is his entity
Thank God

From the earth where we live
To all the stars
They are in his blessings
Thank God, Thank God

Myles W. Wallace

That Is Why I Cut Him

I was standing in line
At the Bonanza Cafe
When the fellow in front of me
Purposely invaded my space

The cashier lady asked
If we were together
To certain people that is something
You should not say-ever

With a look of humiliation
He made an aggressive move
I backed off . . .
I was cool

We each paid for our dinners
And found places to sit down
Out the corner of my eye
I saw "tough guy" stand up
To circle around

He passed by
While giving me the evil eye
I reached for my fork
I already had my knife
Just in case this joker was
Looking for a fight

He came near me again
This time he sneered and
Swiped my chair
That's why I cut him
Long, deep, wide and continuously

He swung again
That's why I cut him
Long, deep, wide and consecutively
From front to end

That Night

That night when I met you
I could not think of
Words to say
You took the breath from me
With your awesome way

You were a magnificent gem
An overpowering feeling
I was captured by your beauty
My heart was revealing

How could you have
Such an effect on me
It doesn't really matter
You just made me so very happy

That night I knew you would be
My one and only love
Heaven must have sent you
From high above

You are so special
Your sweetness is always near
To be with you is ecstasy
I always want you here

Myles W. Wallace

That's When I Fell In Love With You

When you smiled—I spoke
I had a warm feeling
For sure I knew
That's when I fell in love with you

We kissed—my life you became a part
There was never doubt
In my heart
That's when I fell in love with you

All of my thoughts
Belong to you
We will be together-forever
You are so fresh, so new
That's when I fell in love with you

Everytime I see your face
You give my life new meaning
Of you and of you
I am continuously dreaming
That's when I fell in love with you

That's Your Problem

If you don't like the way I walk
That's your problem
If you don't like the way I talk
That's your problem
If you can't stand the way I act
That's your problem
If you dislike the color of my flesh
That's your problem

Counselling won't solve
Your pent-up inhibitions
You are the root of
Your depressed condition

The world doesn't treat you right
That's your problem
You don't have any friends
That's your problem
You weren't born with a silver spoon
That's your problem
Your relatives don't understand
That's your problem

Get yourself together
Stand up and be a woman or a man
Stop blaming others
Life is a better plan

The Candlelight Is Tears To My Eyes

I look at the dining table
Two candles are glowing . . .

Dinner is freshly set
The arrangement is gourmet style
Catered for you, my guest

The food begins to whither
The candles are dim . . .

You never show
My head droops
Just like the roses

The candlelight is tears in my eyes
Eyes that once burned bright
The candlelight is tears in my eyes
It was my only light

The wine sits chilled
Ready to be served
It is left unopened
No footsteps I heard

My door you never enter
To grace my home
I am so cold and all alone

The candlelight is tears in my eyes
Tears that just won't fade away
The candlelight is tears in my eyes
My love shined for you, everyday

The Climax Of Our Love Was The Highlight Of My Life

It came like a bang
With the roar of a lion
My being felt uplifted
And my mind was on cloud nine

We reached our plateau
Just about simultaneously
It was so complete and satisfying
And we came with such spontaneity

The climax of our love
Was the highlight of my life
The climax of our love
Came with no sacrifice

There was an eruption
Of our innermost emotions
There was so much compassion
With love, dedication and devotion

The pinnacle of our desires
The explosion of our intimacy
Was coupled with pure joy
Which was of immense intensity

The climax of our love
Was the highlight of my life
The climax of our love
Was the flame of delight

Myles W. Wallace

The Credit Belongs To You

You brought yourself
Into the present
From out of the past
Happiness will be yours
Now to last

The darkness you saw
Changed to light
You took steps forward
Never to look back

I want to give credit
Where credit is due
The credit, my darling
Belongs to you

There was unhappiness
There were ups and downs
Now you can smile
You turned heartache around

You have taken life
Into your own hands
Now, sweetheart
You possess the master plan

I want to give credit
Where credit is due
Because, my love
It was all you

The Handwriting Is On The Wall

The handwriting is on the wall
It says: I love you
The handwriting is on the wall
I place no one above you

I could write you a letter
Each and every day
But I want the world to know
You are my one and only lady

I could hire a skywriter
To display your hearts' worth
I want you to know
My love for you is down to earth

The handwriting is on the wall
It says: I love you
The handwriting is on the wall
Shows my love is true

I could send you a telegram
Or show my love on television
My feeling for you is
Not bounded by commercialism

I could pass you a note
Like we did when we were in school
What I feel for you
Applies to no rules

The handwriting is on the wall
It says: I love you
The handwriting is on the wall
Is more than brand news

I could display my love on a highway sign
Even on a billboard
The need I have for you
No picture could ever hold

The handwriting is on the wall
It says: I love you
The handwriting is on the wall
Certifies love for me and you

The History of Love

For human beings, love started with Adam and Eve
Passed between generations, for you and me

I want love to grow, through our children and kin
I want love to blossom, continue till this world ends

The history of love, began with time
It was made for every man, woman and child

Love is the way we express that we care
It is more than, having an affair

There are deep emotions, for the one you are involved
You show them by saying, I need you around

The history of love will continue, if we want it that way
It will last forever, let's start today

Myles W. Wallace

The Human Side

He always looks angry
She never smiles
They both act tough
From the other side of town

We are all uniquely different
Peculiarly—we are the same
We all have a destiny
In life's enigmatic game

No matter how adverse you are
Your human side will shine through
Most of us have a sense of decency
The human side is proof

You may be down to no good
At home there may be a
Husband, wife or kids
You will shield them from trouble
Because you are involved with it

With your double-dealing
There is a strong possibility
You will be caught
That is when you realize
Life is only a bout

Inside your head
A solution is contained
The human side is real
Your heart frames
The human side you feel

The Power Of Belief

Believe in God
Believe in yourself
Believe in your mother
Believe in your dad

Believe in good
Believe in love
Believe in achievement
Believe in prayer

The power of belief
Will make you a winner
You are sure to score
From the very beginning

The power of belief
Will see you through
It is something we all have
Just look inside of you

Myles W. Wallace

The Price of Fame

Can't go where you want
Or eat when you please
The world is yours'
Into it you squeeze

People you don't know
Want to hug and kiss
Your life belongs to others
Something is amiss

The price of fame
Can bring on drugs
The price of fame
To do what you love

It is lonely at the top
In a room by yourself
The applause is locked out
Which is your self-respect

You see yourself on television
Imagining it's not you
In your mind
You know the truth

The price of fame
Can drive you to the brink
The price of fame . . .
Stop and think

The Tomb Of The Unknown Soldier

From the leading war
And all that followed
Had their time and space

For this lunacy to still exist
Means the world didn't learn its' lesson
In the first place

Men plucked from their homes
Shipped to far away lands
Forever, most are gone

The tomb of the unknown soldier
Every country has one
The tomb of the unknown soldier
Parents' son

Irrational conflicts resolved nothing
They did more harm than good
Their primitive purposes were
The destruction of manhood

Women in combat
Caught in this senseless mayhem
The bearers of our children
Wouldn't be able to give a second chance

The tomb of the unknown soldier
Please don't make another
The tomb of the unknown soldier
We can't replace our sisters and brothers

Myles W. Wallace

The War That Never Existed—Viet Nam

Viet Nam came
Viet Nam went
It touched us all
-Sordid event

It plucked us from our youths
Some gave their lives
We all wore uniforms
Most not desiring

Viet Nam—the war that never existed
We erase from our memories
Viet Nam, the war—rightly resisted
We go on remembering

Scars remain
Open wounds
What about other countries
They fought and grieve too

A millennium it may take
To purge all the shame
This involvement
Should have never taken place

Viet Nam—the war that never existed
Human lives it took away
Viet Nam—the conflict we should not have entered
We bear the blame

The Weapons Of Love

Some people favor weapons of war
I choose the weapons of love
You will know why
As you read my piece

The weapons of war
Tear down what has been built
With the weapons of love
You can only go uphill

The weapons of war
Only destroy
The weapons of love
Permit inner calm

With the weapons of war
There is always turmoil
Weapons of love are
Sanctioned from above

The weapons of war
Cause nothing but disaster
Weapons of love bring
Happiness—everlasting

The weapons of war
Frequently bear pain
With the weapons of war
Joy remains

I bring you the weapons of love

There Are Two Sides To Every Story

There are two sides to every story
There are two sides to everything we do

Most couples have arguments
As we recently did
I admit I was wrong for
The things I said
If you would just face the fact
I was out of my head

Sometimes, by mistake, we hurt the person
That we are close to
It would hurt me even more
If I lost you

I want you to forgive and forget
For our love to be best
But, you act like we have never met

Everyone makes mistakes
I did not realize
This one would lead to heartache

I am asking you for another chance
Please don't tell me there is no last

Don't go and leave me this way
This is too great a price to pay

There are two sides to every story
There are two sides to everything we do
I love you so much sweetheart
I will do anything to be with you

There Is Always Someone Else

Stalking in shadows
Scoping your love
Anticipating the opportunity
To seize your heart

He waits for the moment
That your foot may slip
That's when he moves in
So he can rip

There is always someone else
You better believe it
There is always someone else
Can't you feel it

Sly and slick
He has no name
Make a mistake
He strikes with a bang

Your next door neighbor
The good fellow at work
It might be a friend
Anywhere he could lurk

There is always someone else
Don't ever doubt
There is always someone else
You will be without

Myles W. Wallace

There's Is No Better Love
Than Making Love
To The One I Love

Stop a moment
Think about what I say
Oh, yes you will recall
Good memories never go away . . .

I remember that special person
With whom I first made love
There was music in the air
Wonderful fragrances
Bells from high above

That first precious kiss
The scintillating touch
It was a beautiful feeling
Savoring the moment
I couldn't get enough

There is no better love
Than making love
To the one I love
It is sweeter than the truth

There is no better love
Than making love
To the one I love
It is better than brand new

I grasp seconds to dream
About those first moments of pleasure
The world seems insignificant
Very far away
By comparison

As we lay in each other's arms
I want to never leave
I wish that ecstacy never ends
It was like the start of creation
I am adam, she is eve

It is paradise on earth
We treasure this unique hour
There is no tearing us apart
The universe does not have the power

There is no better love
Than making love
To the one I love
I let my heart be the judge

There is no better love
Than making love
To the one I love
I have let my story be heard

Things Have got To Get Better

Things have got to get better
That's all I ever hear
Sometimes it doesn't even matter
Meaningless words, year after year

Faded phrases, I can do without
Give me a chance, I'll make it on my own
Some people want to keep me down
I don't need anybody to pave the road

Things have got to get better
They can't get any worse
They've got their hands in my pockets
That's where it really hurts

Sit back and wait
And they say you'll get what you deserve
All my life I've been patient
Yeah, they've really got their nerve

Congress had to pass more laws
I've been here all my years
Poor me, first to serve, first to fight
I helped build this country
With blood, sweat and tears

Revolution may not be possible
But, I've got to escape these conditions
My motto is: Praise the good book
And bring your munitions

Things have got to get better
Wiser words could not have been said
Day in and day out
That's all I hear
Fate only, can decide my destiny
It will be too late then

Things Will Never Be The Way They Used To Be

When we first met
It was like peaches and cream
Now that you're gone
It's like money without the green

It's a very unpleasant situation
I might say
Contrary to your belief
You wanted it this way

It could have been
Sugar and spice
But you went out and took
Someone else's advice

It could have been
Candy and flowers
You came under the influence of
Another's power

It could have been
Cake and ice cream
All it seems to be is
A bad dream

Things will never be
The way they used to be

Things will never be
The way they used to be

Come back, baby
For love we will try
My plea you cannot deny

Things may not be the same
At least, my heart won't be in pain

Love may not be exactly the same
But there is always room for a change

Myles W. Wallace

Think The Best

If you meet a man
Who walks with a crutch
Maybe he is just
Down on his luck

If you meet a lady
You think she's acting shady
Perhaps she is just
Concerned for her baby

Think the best
Don't underestimate
Think the best
Don't be a flake

If you see a child
Not going to school
There's a possibility
He doesn't have any shoes

If you notice a person
Walking back and forth
Maybe this individual
Doesn't have anywhere to go

Think the best
Reach out and help
Think the best
Roles can switch

This Movie Is For You

Hey, my lady
Take my hand
I've got a special movie theater
I want you to go
For the grand opening
—across this land
For your own cinematic picture show

Let me buy you some popcorn
How about a soda-pop
This movie is about you, my dear
In the sold-out palace-house

The curtains part
Lights dim
And the credits begin their roll
The cast is magnificent
As the picture starts
A spectacular sight to behold

There you are, Miss Lady
Sequined, soft-neat
Your moves are so beautiful
Your lines blossom sweet

You are pretty on film
As you are in life
Kissing you on screen
Would be pure delight

You ask me how I made a movie of you
Well my love, I filmed you unaware
I wanted a lot of pictures
The positives were so positive
I wanted the world to share

I filmed you sleeping
An angel you were
I filmed you laughing
Sensuous to me, you occurred
I took frames with friends
You were a stand-out
I shot your mind
You know what life is about

I—highlighted your eyes
Those shining stars
I took flicks of your legs
A model you are
I filmed your hands
A concert pianist's desire
I captured your ways
That make you fine

This movie is for you
Dedicated to your beauty
My movie of you is admiration
That Hollywood could envy

This movie is for you

It was written with passion
About you I feel
Directed with love
That I can't conceal

It was produced by my heart
My vision of you
Edited in my mind
I care only for you

The scenes are for real
Color by technicolor
The story so true
It would be of no other

The orchestra is symphonic
For your soundstage vibes
The narration in tune
To accentuate your life

This movie is for you
Will never end
Though the curtains slowly close
The lights brighten up

This movie is for you
Is just the beginning
Of everything that I feel
You are totally what love is about

This Story Will Never End

Don't close my book
Don't turn your back
Don't hide me in a box
And never unpack

Don't flip my pages
Don't remove your marker
Don't abruptly change subjects
I want to be your main topic

This story will never end
There will be no other
This story will never end
I am not under cover

Don't leave my admiration in the den
Don't pull my affection off the table
Don't declare my devotion obsolete
Like some faded fable

Don't cover my fondness with dust
Don't wedge my tenderness in a jacket
Don't store my kindness on a shelf
Or place my passion in a package

This story will never end
You don't need a library card
This story will never end
My story is my heart

Those Hands And Feet

Your little hands are
So small, so delicate, so neat
And your beautiful legs
Are supported by itsy bitsy feet

Your body, normal it grew
But at the wrists and ankles
It stopped
When people say mini-sized
You know exactly
What they are talking about

Your hands are perfect,
Though midget
Your little feet-
Sitting is their pleasure
Ability did not pass you up
Your pint-sized jewels
Have excelled you in lifes' measures

To kiss every finger, every toe
Is how I fantasize
All of you I will love
One member at a time

Your little hands are
Soft to the touch
Pretty little feet
Cuddle them I must

Time

Time has no beginning
Time will never end
Time can be an enemy
Or it may be a friend

Time is forever
And it can mean never
Time can't be wrong
It is just too clever

Time is a revealer
It can be a healer
Without time
Decision would be without reason

Time changes
It also rearranges
The more it changes
More of it becomes the same

Time is young
Yet it is old
Time moves
Sometimes it molds
At times it's on hold

Time doesn't sound
It goes around
It won't turn back
When it can wear down

Time is the nature of life
It makes the earth revolve
Time can not be controlled
It is universe bound

To Be In Love

To be in love
Truly, a rosy world
To be in love
Verifies you are my girl

As I maturated
Life, I felt passing by
You terminated that process
With your effervescent vibes

Fun—once dull
Now ethereally nice
My former companion, loneliness
Stays hidden from sight

To be in love
What an ecstatic feeling
To be in love
Is minds revealing

My silent telephone
Now vibrantly chimes
When you call
Vivid tones illuminate my mind

Shuttered doors
Are now opened wide
The curtains also parted
For you, my sunshine

To be in love
Is identically satisfying
Being in love
Is effortless compromising

To Smell

MMMMMMMPPM (Inhaling)
AAAAAAAAHH (Exhaling)
To Smell!
Savor the fresh clean air
To Smell!
Touch the atmosphere

Wonderful aromas
Transverse space
Luscious vapors
Fragrant waves

Hot Smells!
Sweet Smells!
Tender Smells!
Spicy Smells!
Tangy Smells!

These are just a few smells
That enter my nasal passage
The excite, titillate, tingle
My mind gets the message

To Smell!
MMMMMMMMPPMMMM!
A vibrant sensation
To Smell!
AAAAAAAAAAHHHH!
Positively invigorating!

Took The words Right Out Of My Mouth

The economy is bad
Jobs are scarce
They forgot the poor
Gave it to the rich

Food is unaffordable
Heat or eat
Gasoline prices—rampant
The democratic process defeated

Took the words right out of my mouth
Degranomics
You took the words right out of my mouth
Degranomics

Social Security is fading
The Stock Market—fluctuating
Financial plans—tumbling
Portfolios, vacillating

Mortgage foreclosures
Skyhigh interest rates
Five-year car notes
From bankruptcy—there is no escape

You took the words right out of my mouth
Degranomics
Took the words right out of my mouth
DEGRANOMICS

Torch

I carry a torch for you, lady
Flames arc high
I carry a torch for you, lady
Sparks strike the sky

Darling you are the most sincere lady
My life has shown
Love burns in my heart
To you I belong

Magic moments we are united
Blaze my mind
Your radiant beauty
Brands lifes' times

I carry a torch for you, lady
Olympic serenade
I carry a torch for you, lady
Liberty day parade

When we embrace
Love starts to warm
Heated undulations
Intense like the sun

You are so sensuous
My brain is fire
Your glowing persona
Fuels my desire

Sugar you will always be
My fervent love, endlessly

I carry a torch for you, lady
Flare bright
I carry a torch for you, baby
Dawn through night

Transparent People

What if people had no skin covering
You could see their hearts
The blood that runs through them
All the internal parts

You will find that people
Are the same inside
That includes their souls
As well as their minds

When you meet humankind
Don't judge how they look
Understanding human beings
Is not like reading books

Think of people being transparent
Then things won't be apparent
Think of others as transparent
And your words won't go errant

People are intricate and complex
Like other forms of life
So, when you look inside
You will see the light

Picture people as transparent
Like they are covered with glass
See people as transparent
And you will discover
Society is the same class

Myles W. Wallace

Trees, Tracks, Water

See the trees
Hear the Brothers
Feel the tracks
There's the Sisters
Near the water
All my children

Trees, tracks, water
Divide and separate
Symbols of no escape

On the other side
Another world
Beer drinking men
Prancing girls
Neither care or worry

Compare the two
Adjacent neighborhoods
Everything is marvelous
Knock on wood

Trees, tracks, water
Mansions and bricks
Wait a minute
I hear ticks

Truck Stop Sally

Five at a time
They rolled in
With the wave of her hand
They were friends

Internationals, Kenwoods
Macks, Peterbilts, Whites
And company men
They stopped by
For live entertainment

Truck Stop Sally
Gives nourishment
Truck Stop Sally
Full of encouragement

This lady is no tramp
Her head is always high
She speaks words of wisdom
To get you through the night

Liquor, drugs
Never touches the stuff
Her goal is life
She cannot get enough

Truck Stop Sally
She is good for 1000 miles
Sally as she like to be called
Always has a smile

Myles W. Wallace

Truth Is Stranger Then Fiction

My baby whispered she loved me
Then she hollered: "I'm going away"
She told me, I didn't deserve her
But she could not bare to stay

She said I was no longer the man for her
She had a dream lover on the side
I didn't want to hear it
Least, it blow my mind

We had just made love that morning
Seemed like for four-hours straight
She said her man gave it to her
Eight-hours, everyday

How could this be, I pondered
A better man than I
Especially when this was supposed to be
My cherry laying beside

I put forth my best rap
Wishing she would give in
She said it was too late for that
And didn't want to hear

I cried myself to sleep
When I awoke—she was gone
She had ransacked for money
Confiscated all her clothes

I immediately called my best friend
Told him what had happened
He said: "I don't understand"

I visited my doctor
Tried to explain the chain of events
He stated: "I'm only a man"

I went by Mamas
She said: "I know you love this girl
You say she rocks your world
But—What I'm about to tell you
May shatter your nerves"

"Sit down son
I see you've got a lot to learn
I know I may sound unconvincing
But the heart of the matter is
Truth is stranger than fiction"

She said: "I'll tell you once again
About your uncertain position
The crux of this unfortunate situation is
Truth is stranger than fiction"

Well, I hadn't heard from my ex
It was going on three months
When I was awaken by the phone
One morning at four o'clock

It was my one-time-use-to-be
She said: "I want to come home
I think I'm in love with you
Can you dig where I'm coming from?"

I told her:
"Woman, you sound like Alice In Wonderland
You better pinch yourself and wake-up
You are living in a world of fairy-tales
And make-believe
You want me to play the role—nut"

With all said; I still dug this lady
But to live with her again
I began reminiscing
All the heartache, all the pain
Truth is stranger than fiction

We have been together a year
She hasn't gone through an act
She says she's so happy to be with me
I still watch my back

Like the Law of Murphy says;
Anything that can go wrong will
It wouldn't sunrise me none
If she came up missing
I'll remember what my Mamma told me:
"Son truth is more stranger than fiction"

So when someone asks me for love's advice
I tell them by life's admission
Follow your heart with caution
Truth is a whole lot more stranger than fiction

Turntable

Turntable, turntable
Spinning around

Turntable, turntable
Producing groovy sounds

Turntable, turntable
Moving back and forth

Turntable, turntable
Continuously on the go

Turntable, turntable
Doing duty
Just like a pro

Turntable
You put on
One heck-of-a-show

Turntable
Fined tuned-
With strobe
Excellent timing
Fast and slow
You've got real power
Always in control

Turntable, turntable
You're the number one component
Don't you know

Twinkle In His Eye

Now he would get mad . . .
Ole dad

Thoughts of father . . .

He is a good ole man
I think of the times
He would use his hand
Ole Dad . . .

He didn't take no mess
Discipline was his rule
He never raised his voice
Wisdom was his tool
Dad wasn't bad
He was just
Ole dad . . .

He would have a twinkle in his eye
No matter how angered he would get
He would have a twinkle in his eye
He was teaching self-respect

The years have melted
I am a man—grown
Even now when I visit
Sitting, he strikes me with awe

We will have a discussion
Most times he's right
I am more than happy
I used his advice

I think
Dad was not all that bad
He is just . . .
Ole Dad

He still has that twinkle in his eye
He is a real man
With that twinkle in his eye
That is my Dad
Ole Dad . . .

Valor

Dignity, integrity, self-respect

You learn to give
And not receive
The truth is better when
You don't deceive

You keep your head high
No matter what situation
It makes you stronger
It is a way of displaying

Valor—Your special tool
Valor—The golden rule

Compassion, patience, unselfishness

Valor may seem old-fashioned
For the world in which we live
It will never become outdated
To do a good deed

Try it once a day
Make it an honor system
You will find that
You enjoy this new condition

Valor—Will keep you atop
Valor—No doubt

Myles W. Wallace

What Do You Do

When pretty turns putty
What do you do
Love should be inside you

When muscle turns to flab
What do you do
Love better be inside you

When intelligence goes zilch
What do you do
Love should be inside you

When your luck is down
And you have no one to look to
You better believe
Love best be inside you

Follow your heart
Love will stay inside you

What Is A Body Without A Mind

What is a mind without a body
What is a body without a mind
I don't want to love one and not the other
I want them both, all the time

You persistently say
I want you only for your body
Me, you don't trust
As two human beings in love
We do what we must

You are more to me than just a female
You are love and affection combined
This is why you are more than a body
I want you to be all mine

Your body is beautiful
This I admit
Your mind makes you even more beautiful
Lovely as your kiss

Please don't ever think
I want to love you
Just for your body alone
To do something like that . . .
I would rather leave you alone

Myles W. Wallace

What Is Worth Having—Is Worth Waiting For

We met no long ago
Your life I wanted a part
You told me to wait, because
I could not have your heart

I was persistent
Never, would I give up
You began to give in
You said: "You liked me a lot"

What is worth having—is worth waiting for
My life I have wanted you
What is worth having—is worth waiting for
Surely you are my dream come true

We are getting to know each other better
Of me, you have become fonder
Love continuously blossoms
No time to ponder

Now our hearts beat one
We are hand in hand
I will never leave you
I want to be your one and only man

What is worth having—is worth waiting for
These words I have found true
What is worth having—is worth waiting for
You are my living proof

What Would I Do

Baby, I don't know what I would do
If I didn't have you

I don't know what I would do
If you said you didn't need me

Baby, I don't know where I would be
If you were not the one for me

You are my one and only desire
You set my soul on fire

The love I have for you is so strong
Between us there could be no wrong

This element called time separates
I know in the future you wait

The day will come
I will hold you in my arms

You are my special girl
The only one in this whole world

Baby I don't know what I would do
If I didn't have you

Whatever She Is, She Is Mine

They call her flighty
They say she dates many men
They say she has a book of numbers
Of nothing but male friends

Sometimes she arrives home late
Been gone too long
Most times when I call
A recorder answers the phone

Whatever she is, she is mine
I love this woman
Whatever she is, she is mine
I want no other

I enjoy her company
She always treats me nice
If there is a problem
She will seek my advice

She does not hurt the eyes
She has a beautiful smile
She tells people
I am her man around town

Whatever she is, she is mine
I am going to keep her
Whatever she is, she is mine
I will never leave her

When The Glitter Is Gone

When the curtain is down
And your youth is done
To who will you turn
To hear your song

You say you will wait
Till the time comes
By then it will be too late
If you would slow down a minute
Just to think

When the glitter is gone
There will be no escape
When the glitter is gone
The way this game is played

Remember the times
You are fancy free
That is your way to live
Oh! So short! So brief!

Maturation will set in
You will miss the beat
Then you will realize
Your life is so incomplete

When the glitter is gone
The fountain will spring no more
When the glitter is gone
You will know the score

Myles W. Wallace

Who Are The Faceless People

Lurking in the shadows
They assassinate, they destroy
Your life and my life
Are insignificant toys

Plotting—scheming
Is their fame
They never lose
With their secret game

Who are the faceless people
Let us see your faces
Who are the faceless people
Come out of your hiding places

They camouflage themselves
As the mentally unfit
Until they accomplish
Their dastardly tricks

Into the woodwork
They swiftly return
Taking no responsibility
For their despicable purloins

Who are the faceless people
Stand up and be counted
Who are the faceless people
They public can do without

Why

You don't cheat
You never contrive
You told me goodbye
Why

You don't hurt
You never lie
My love you won't try
Why

You never run
You don't hide
My heart you deny
Why

You don't trick
You aren't sly
You made me feel good inside
Why

You are pretty
A prize
Now, it's the end of the line
Why?

I want you to be mine

With The Quickness

When you call my name
I'll be there with the quickness
To play your game
With the quickness

I'm ready like Freddy
Cause I drink seven-up
I'll be there directly
You sweet buttercup

When you want me to come
I'll be there with the quickness
If you want a run
I'll do it with the quickness

I'm fast as a rabbit
Going down a greased laundry shoot
I'll be with you
Before the light goes kaput

You want money
I'll bring it to you with the quickness
I'll give you a lot honey
With the quickness

I'm like barbecue
Hot off the grill
A rolling stone
Going downhill
Whatever you want
I'll pay the bill

When you want good love
I'll be there with the quickness
For delicious kisses and hugs
I'll come with the quickness

I'm just like peas
Steaming in the pot
Sure enough smoking
Cause the water is hot

I'll be your johnny-on-the-spot
With the quickness
Your special piece of the rock
With the quickness

Xmas Blues

They have finished shopping
The crowd is gone
With one wreath
I am all alone

Christmas comes
Just once a year
For me, that is too much
Too much fear

Xmas Blues
Keep the title short
Xmas Blues
HHMMM, whiskey of sorts

People say
I'm a scrooge
They just don't understand
How to lose

One week from now
I will wait for Xmas
To come again
What the heck
Have a Happy New Year

Xmas Blues
At no time do I accept
Xmas Blues
I never forget

Yes You Are

You are my baby
Oh yes you are
Yes you are

You are my baby
Oh yes you are

You are baby
Whether near or far
Yes you are
You are, you are

You are my lady
Oh yes you are
Yes you are

You are my lady
Yes you are
You are, you are

You are my light
You are, you are
Oh yes, yes you are

You are my day
You are, you are
You are

You are my sun
You are, you are
You are

You are my baby
You are, you are
Oh yes you are
Yes you are
Oh yes you are

Myles W. Wallace

You Are The One For Me

Like the dress I brought you on
Our shopping spree
You are the one for me

The diamond ring I gave you
Sparkling
You are the one for me

You are a light that shines so bright
A star that fills the night

You are beautiful—tranquility
You are the one for me

From a far away view
You were my true love, I knew

You are the one for me
Astrology
Taurus—harmony

What better combination could love be
You are sincere, so sweet
Yes, you are the one for me

You Are Too Pretty, To Be So Fine

When we first met
I blurted: "You're sweet"
You spoke so sensuously

Your complimentary beauty
Completely—overpowered me

We became lovers
I knew marriage—for sure
But, you departed with no explanation
I felt so insecure

Fate crossed our lives, surprisingly—again
But, instead of being sweethearts
You said: "We're just friends"

During our separation
A change you went through
Now, when we see each other
You're on a different avenue

You conversation is abstract
An attempt to act hep
Crammed in your micro-mini
You strut with a switch

Sarcasm has replaced
Your optimism for life
Your natural loving fragrance
No more than watered spice

Your once beautiful smile
Has turned into a pout
You even hit on me
Before, I asked you out

Home, you never stay
Always on the go
You can't stand to listen
Everything you know

Lady, you're too pretty, to be so fine
You're always on my mind
Darling, you're too pretty to be so fine
Sugar, you're still my kind

You hurt me so
Pretending you're not
If you just accept my love
I know it will be
The key to your lock

Let me wine you, dine you
Do whatever I need to win
I want to be your man
You and I as one, again

If it's something I've done
If I led you astray
I'll make it up in love
For you, always

Baby, you're too pretty to be so fine
I realize, we change with time
Honey, you're too pretty to be so fine
Oh, how I wish!
You were still—mine

You Bring Out The Teenage Love In Me

Whenever I'm with you
I think of what teenagers do

Wherever I'm kissing you
Love is blossoming new

When we walk, holding hands
I feel eighteen, all over again

When I call and hear your voice
You're sweet sixteen and oh—so choice!

You bring out the teenage love in me
Only you and candy could be so sweet

You bring out the teenage love in me
Age has no number for you and me

With you, all I have to do is sit and talk
Love is captured, everywhere we walk

We don't need popcorn at the show
Our love won't let go

We watch the stars, while on the beach
Only with you, they don't seem out of reach

You are what keeps the world young
High above, is from where you come

You bring out the teenage love in me
Like a flower blooming in the spring

You bring out the teenage love in me
Into my life, the sun you bring

Myles W. Wallace

You Can't Predict Luck

One day you wake up
Go out and find a dollar
The next day you oversleep
And can't even borrow a quarter

You go through winter
Not even catch a cold
Here comes summer
You start to blow your nose

You can't predict luck
Like finding a four leaf clover
You can't predict luck
It will never get you over

You'll be out and see
The coat you always wanted
The next day you go back
The salesperson sold it

You invest one-hundred dollars
To try to make a mint
When the results come in
You owe one-hundred-one dollars
Plus fifty-cents

You can't predict luck
It's like an unlucky rabbit's foot
You can't predict luck
Few times you win
Most times you just get took

You Didn't Have To Go

You didn't have to leave me
You didn't have to go
You didn't have to leave me
You didn't have to go

It never occurred to me
I hurt you so

Time after time
I made mistakes
But this situation
I did not anticipate

It was just the other day
You said we could compromise
Now that you are gone
I am so surprised

I want to make ends meet
All I get is defeat

You didn't have to leave me
You didn't have to go
You didn't have to leave me
You didn't have to go

If life is a chance
Please come back to me
The feeling I have . . .
You are the breath of me

Myles W. Wallace

You Have Got someone To Turn To

Sometimes you feel as if
You have lost your best friend
And no one seems to care
Your life is upside down
Dreams have turned to despair

No matter what you do
Situations never seem to go right
When you are most in need of solutions
There is no one to give advice

You have got someone to turn to
You can call, ring or write
You have got someone to turn to
Ask for him day and night

You get down on your knees to pray
Your prayers seem to go unanswered
Happiness looks as if it escapes you
The joy that you want everlasting

The harder you try for your goal
The less you seem to succeed
It is one heartache after another
You say it cannot be for real

You have got someone to turn to
To set your life free
You have got someone to turn to
That someone is me

You Made Me Whole

I was like an explosion
I lost control
When you came into my life

Made me whole

I was trying to make adjustments
To changes in my life
When it caved in
Became self-sacrifice

Bits and pieces of me
Were all over
When I unraveled
I've been told
Life is a gamble

You made me whole

Out of light you appeared
No blue smoke or mirrors
So for real, so serious

Like a sculptor
You reshaped what was leftover
Molded me like clay
I feel like four-leaf clover

You made me whole

Myles W. Wallace

Your Love Brings Out The Best In Me

With you I am always happy
I am never sad
You keep me smiling
I am so glad

I walk with pride
On top of the world
I constantly boast
You are my girl

Your love brings out the best in me
You earned an "A"
Your love brings out the best in me
With a gold star behind your name

I treat my friends
With more respect
It is not in my heart
People to reject

Work is great
School is a thrill
I am king of the mountain
I don't worry about bills

Your love brings out the best in me
Thank you, baby
Your love brings out the best in me
I love your way

Your Love Is—So Dear In My heart

We make love—I remember
I don't forget
It's no hurry session
There are never any regrets

When lovemaking is completed
Love is never gone
Though we part
Your sweetness lingers on

Your love is—so dear in my heart
Close as our minds
Your love is—so dear in my heart
We never say goodbye

As we lay
Soon you will leave
The time comes
You are always in my dream

When I go
It is never to stay
Though, it seems for a lifetime
I want you always

Your love is—so dear in my heart
Without it life would not be fair
Your love is—so dear in my heart
With you, love is everywhere

Your Love Is Truth

Darling, it would take hours of
Your precious time, to tell you
How much I am in love with you
You mean so many things to me
Words could not describe
How much I adore you too

In our years together
Not once have you stood me up
Nor have you put me down
In the worst of times
You—somehow—managed a smile

You always do the things
You promised you would do
Without a doubt
You are always on time
With loving good news

Your love is truth
Straight from the heart
Your love is truth
I love being a part

Not a day passes
That you remember me in some special way
Whether it is a call or card
You have always got
Something sweet to say

You have aura around you
That accents your magnetic vibes
With your angel touch
Your joy for life
You light up my mind

You are so nice to me
To others you are the same
If anyone needs a friend
Or a hand to hold
You are there without refrain

Your love is truth
It rings soft and clear
You are living proof
I am very happy you are here

Myles W. Wallace

Your Love Makes My day

When I rise in the morning
Feeling like I want a cup of tea
And a warm piece of cake
I don't need those ingredients
Your love makes may day

I try to read the newspaper
To catch up with current events
I don't want that play
Your understanding personality is it
Your love makes my day

I go to work and the supervisor says:
"We have lots of overtime"
I tell him—"No way!"
I have got to go home to
That beautiful lady of mine
Your love makes my day

After the ups and downs
Of everyday life
I can't wait to see your lovely face
Wishing I didn't have to go away
Your love makes my day

Your Love Rings A Bell

The first day of our romance
Down I fell
I was t.k.o.'d
Your love rings a bell

Just like in school
At the start of class
I'm filled with joy
Your love rings a bell

When the telephone chimes
To hear your sweet voice is swell
I immediately react
Your love rings a bell

Like a strongman's mallet
At a county summer fair
Your love is solid
Your love rings a bell

Like the cathedral tower
At sounding spells
I respond spontaneously
Your love rings a bell

I wish for us to be together
I need your sweet love near
My heart seconds that devotion
Its beat is crystal clear

Just like a typewriter
At the completion of a line
Your love will always be
Right on time

Your love is the best
You make my life jell
You are my true love
Your love rings a bell

Myles W. Wallace

Your Picture Is Worth (1000 Words)

I look at your photo
And smile
I haven't heard from you
In a while

If the telephone doesn't ring
You are always close
When my door doesn't open
I want you most

Your picture is worth (1000 words)
With it near
Your picture is worth (1000 words)
I have you here

You left for a journey
To become in touch with life
In my heart
I know you're right

One day you will return
Until then, I will remain composed
In the mean time
Your photograph shows

Your picture is worth (1000 words)
It is all I need
Your picture is worth (1000 words)
To keep me company

You've Got To Love Somebody

You think you've got it made, yet
You come home all to yourself
You're in love with material possessions
You've placed your heart on a shelf

You can go out and buy
Anything that you want
There's no price tag on love
But your mind tells you don't

You've got to love somebody
You have to hold and squeeze someone
You've got to love somebody
Or life is no fun

You can go to fancy restaurants
And other stylish places
Inside you hurt because all you see
Are smiling faces

You try to get away from it all
There is no running away
You need that special person
Just to make your day

You've got to love somebody
Don't put it off until tomorrow
You've got to love somebody
Without love, there is only sorrow